MOM AF

Christine Michel Carter

To request authorization, please contact Minority Woman Marketing. Please outline the specific material involved, the proposed medium, if applicable, the number of copies, as well as the purpose of the use.

christinemichelcarter.com

2019 Minority Woman Marketing LLC

Library of Congress Cataloging-in-Publication Data

https://lccn.loc.gov/2019915495

Carter, Christine Michel. MOM AF / Christine Michel Carter. Baltimore, MD : Sarsins LLC, 2019.

Pages cm

ISBN: 9781734122701

Formatting by Self-Publishing Services, LLC
www.selfpublishingservices.com

Edited by Aja Dorsey Jackson
Cover Photographer Renee Hollingshead
Disclaimer
First Printing Edition, 2019

WHAT PEOPLE ARE SAYING ABOUT CHRISTINE

"Thanks for doing the work you do. It's so important to amplify the working mom realities not only to normalize the struggles we all go through, but to develop, implement, and grow strategies to combat them."

—Sara Lewis, Founder and CEO of The Bond Project

"Christine Michel Carter is a writer, speaker, and marketing consultant who knows exactly what brands are looking for when it comes to targeting the 'mom' demographic."

—Romper

DEDICATED TO THE ONES I LOVE...HEYYYYY

The Holy Trinity:
To Edna, for teaching me the lesson.
To Maya, for allowing me to apply the lesson.
And to Marsha, for not letting me give up in the middle.

CONTENTS

ABOUT THE AUTHOR

Christine Michel Carter's voice is one that is vital for all to hear. Her authentic, unique, and insightful writing elevates whatever conversation she is a part of to a level that transforms the listener. She courageously tells stories from a perspective that gives the reader the license to become more of who they are in this world.

—Alicia Wilson, Johns Hopkins University

Featured in The New York Times, Christine Michel Carter is the #1 global voice for working moms. Called "the mom of mom influencers," "the exec inspiring millennial moms," and "the voice of millennial moms", Christine clarifies misconceptions about working mom consumers for brands and serves as an amplifier of their personal truths. From delivering consumer insights and brand marketing content to helping HR and diversity teams attract and retain these hardworking professionals, Christine works with advertising agencies, research firms and companies to ensure they're at the forefront of the minds of female consumers.

Her insights have been included by authors in their books, and Christine's own bestselling children's book Can Mommy Go To Work? was ranked as an "empowering book" and a "life changing book to guide feminist parenting." Christine also contributes to several global digital publications, including Forbes, TIME, Harper's BAZAAR and Parents.

Because of her digital presence and work with mom influencers, Christine was asked by Senator Kamala Harris to support the awareness of the Maternal CARE Act, a personal issue also close to her heart. The creator of Mompreneur and Me, Christine has introduced the first national mommy and me professional development networking event that has garnered the attention of Adweek and Entrepreneur as well as global brands like McDonald's and Tessemae's.

INTRODUCTION:

WE AIN'T F***ING WAKE UP LIKE THIS.

"Being our messy, imperfect, authentic selves helps create a space where others feel safe to be themselves, too. Your vulnerability can be a gift to others, how badass is that?"

—b.oakman, If You Needed A Reason to Be You

The back cover may have told you about who I am, but you may still be wondering why I actually wrote MOM AF.

I'm striving to be perfect, but am by no means close to it. After all, society demands so much of us. In today's world, many of us are on the journey to becoming health-conscious women. We desire to be the best moms, partners, and professionals. But we keep running on caffeine, chaos and cuss words. Tireless doubts overwhelm every decision we make.

See? You are not alone.

There are millions of us. We're flawed. We're unpolished. We AIN'T wake up like this.

The last thing you need in your life is a guidebook on how to be a mother and career woman, so don't expect to find it here.

Once you dig into this book's pages, it will become evident: I am a **MESS**. As a wife and mother, I am oblivious to the chaos controlling my life, applying band-aid after band-aid to large unaddressed wounds. Go ahead; laugh at my missteps. Cry at my passion (and disdain) for my children. Question why I can't see the forest for the trees...because I want you to see how we all so quickly become consumed with trying to survive daily that we totally miss the bigger picture.

I always debate and doubt my right to be an author, questioning if I am valid enough to share my struggles with you. But I've come to the conclusion that my validity is my experience; my lacking perfection. And it's precisely why I wrote this novel. Sounds strange? Check it:

> *"Repeat after me: I am allowed to be BOTH a work in progress AND help others grow at the same time. I refuse to wait until I believe I'm perfect or someone else has deemed me worthy of impacting others. I am unapologetically accepting of a life of massive growth & improvement."*

> *—source unknown*

I may not be a celebrity, socialite, or a billion-dollar entrepreneur at the end of the day; but still, I'm full of passion. I want to see working moms like me–my tribe–represented in a positive light. Before starting this book, I was getting great feedback from my articles, in particular, the ones which dealt with the pain points of being a working millennial mom. Mothers from Alaska to Australia were finding my personal anecdotes and experiences relatable, funny, and honest. Their feedback makes me feel that there's a void missing in these women's lives, that they need a release. Working mothers need to see someone else **NOT** pretending to be perfect while straining their fucked-up life through Snapchat filters and forced smiles.

These were wives who questioned their marriages. Professionals who quit jobs they hated only to suffer emotionally and financially because of it. Women who needed a space offline where they could connect and find empathy. And mothers who still spank their kids when they're acting a fool (instead of "counting to three").

Humans. Go figure.

What you do need (and what I offer to you) are honesty and companionship. You're reading this book because you don't want to feel regret. And believe me, you are not alone. This is a sister circle in a book; it is about YOU. You're going to hear the story of a woman you've never met, but who might be just like you. My spirit is fueled by you. I'm a badass bitch now, but you'll soon discover that means being a boss in some areas, just okay in a few more, and downright fucked-up in the rest.

Above all, I hope that this book will help you rediscover yourself again—outside of being a mom. I hope it boosts your confidence and makes you feel great in your own skin. It's okay to want to reclaim your life. To regain your strength, your sexy, and your sanity. It's my story, but it was written with you in mind, mama, because I, too, sometimes let other forces take it over. At the end of the day, we're all just striving for balance while raising these little turds; we have more similarities than differences.

You may not be perfect at the end of this book, but hopefully, I can help you be present.

Happy reading.

Christine

CHAPTER ONE

THE F***ING TRIP TO CHICK-FIL-A

6:20 AM: Get the kids dressed & James out the door! 💀🗯️

"FUUUCCCKKKK!!!!"

I softly mouthed the obscenity, dragging it out for three seconds.

My bare foot throbbed in pain. I didn't see Rubble, one of my two-year-old son's plastic Paw Patrol figurines, because I was too busy scrolling my iPhone and looking for my Amtrak email confirmation. (After you have kids, all curse words have to be uttered behind their backs, in your mind, or mouthed softly. Of course, this infuriated me even more.)

"Mommy, you sqwuishe Rubble. He's sqwuishe," my son West barely said. But I speak two-year-old fluently, so I knew what he meant.

I cracked a smile at his statement of the obvious, but as I limped into my bedroom, the smile turned to a groan. "Maybe if these

FUCKING kids put away their GOT DAMN toys, my FUCKING foot wouldn't be in pain!"

I woke up on time every morning. The worst-case scenario is plus or minus 10 minutes. But every morning, everyone *else* in the house would expect 10, 15, or 20 extra minutes to sleep. As if we had the luxury of time on THIS particular morning. Thirty minutes later, their routine began. And every damn day, I could count on all of them (my husband James, my five-year-old daughter Maya, and West) to get their asses ready as if they forgot what actions they were supposed to take to get ready from when they did the same thing on the *previous* day.

If I was late for that motherfuckin' train, somebody was gonna GET it!

My thoughts were interrupted by another offspring.

"Wait! I can't find Anna," Maya whined. "I had her in bed last night, and now I can't find her!" She conjured the acting skills necessary to win a landslide Oscar—sobbing and panting in tandem. I wanted to yell, "WHY THE HELL DOES ANNA'S WHEREABOUTS MATTER AT THIS MOMENT? GET OUT THE DAMN HOUSE! YOU CAN'T EVEN TAKE THE TOY TO SCHOOL, ANYWAY!" Instead, I gritted my teeth.

"Mommy will look for Anna and have her on your bed when you come home."

Every morning...the same.

First, their procrastinating asses started by moving slower than King Syrup poured from a bottle in the midst of a blizzard. Then, they finished with a rush through the hallway like the theme song from *The Benny Hill Show* was playing in the background. Even when I scheduled "what ifs" for the pussy-footing posse—or as I endearingly liked to call that time block, "Fuck Up Time"—we were always late. In the course of the morning routine, Maya always lost an Elsa sneaker, West always wanted two bowls of oatmeal, and James always needed to use the bathroom RIGHT before we walked out the door.

One morning, I stuck West in my bed because we had a few moments to spare. As he laid there, I noticed he had a mild fever and was panting in my ear. I leaned into him, looking at his face while muttering to myself: *I forgot what this means when he starts panting like crazy. What is—*

and he vomited in my face.

What could I do but stand there and take it? If I moved, vomit would just spread all over the bedspread. All I could do was what I have always done: curse in my head with rage. *"What the fuck is it with these children? All this whining and coughing and shit. Do they have polio? Am I raising kids in the middle of the fucking Great Depression? Fuck!"*

I continuously searched for ways to make the morning routine run smoother. I once even tried implementing a routine with Maya I found on one of those "perfect mom" websites, hoping to expedite the disastrous morning routine in the Carter household. I *know* you KNOW what a "perfect mom" website is. A landing page of lies devoted to a gospel preached by other mothers. Its primary creation is to make you feel like a piece of shit.

This particular routine was posted by one of those dumb ass mothers who patiently let their kids get dressed by themselves in the morning, considering it the perfect opportunity for them to gradually master getting ready independently. It suggested something like this:

> *Open the child's door in the morning, turning on the hall light while you get ready. The light and noise should help to wake them up slowly. Once you've gotten yourself ready for the morning, go in and pick them up out of bed. Carry them to a comfortable place to sit and cuddle. (They're most likely still dozing or just waking up.) While holding them, talk about what they dreamt last night, what*

they want to do today or anything that's happening with friends or school or fun, for the next five to ten minutes. Focus on fun stuff, to look forward to during the day! You'll find they'll join the conversation in no time! Then, afterward, play a game around getting dressed. Pretend it's a race! Competition is a fantastic motivator for children.

When I initially read it—with a straight face mind you—I thought, "Are you fucking serious? I. Don't. Have. The. Time. For. That. Shit." Nevertheless, I gave it a try. The routine actually played out with Maya as follows:

Open the child's door in the morning, turning on the hall light while you get ready. The light and noise should help to wake them up slowly.

"Turn off the LIGGGHHHTTT!!" Maya screamed as she rolled the covers back over her face, sleeping for another 10 minutes.

Once you get yourself ready for the morning, go in and pick them up out of bed. Carry them to a comfortable place to sit and cuddle. (They're most likely still dozing or just waking up.) While holding them, talk about what they dreamt last night, what they want to do today or anything that's happening with friends or school or fun, for the next 5-10 minutes.

Awww.

Maya doesn't answer a damn question I ask. Not even, "Get up and go to the bathroom. Do you *wanna* pee on yourself when you get to school?"

Then, afterward, play a game around getting dressed—pretend it's a race! Competition is a fantastic motivator for children.

I dressed her brother first and yelled from his room, excitedly, "Look, Maya! West is getting dressed really fast! He's a big boy! He's about to beat you because he's almost ready!"

"Getting dressed is not a competition, Mommy," Maya quipped. "You shouldn't rush, rush, rush through it," she said, imitating someone running as she spoke. "It's not like that."

Well, damn. That worked like gangbusters.

"JAMES!" I yelled.

Ah, James. My hubby and baby daddy. James (also known as Handsome McHandsomekins) was with whom I legally shared the responsibilities of our children. (And shit, I should damn well have had his help as he was the other human being who contributed in their conception.) He was tall and dark, and I'd given him the nickname Handsome McHandsomekins when we first started dating in college. He'd kept a lean, fit frame since those days, and passed his long limbs down to our children. When we walked down the street, he was a direct contrast to my stubby, tan appearance.

Like every other morning in my life, from whatever ceiling I was currently under, I hollered, "James, can you help me OUT here? I gotta get to the train station!"

"I don't have time! I have to get ready TOO!" he shouted back from the basement with his husky voice. No fail, James was, without question, the love of my life and my soul mate. Most importantly, he was my king. But in the decade I'd been living with the man, he had not adapted to my need for morning organization, routine, and structure. Sometimes I felt my role as a *domestic concierge* didn't start when I had children; it began 11 years ago with James.

I huffed. "But I do? I have a meeting as soon as I hit the office!"

I started frantically squeezing my giant fun bags into a size medium sports bra. James sauntered up the basement stairs and into the kitchen. "BABE, WHERE ARE THE PLASTIC BAGS? I need to put Maya's graham crackers in a baggie so..."

Now I was done.

This man spent so little time in the kitchen that he didn't even know where most of the groceries belonged. In 11 years, he had cooked 10 times (and that's a generous number). Five of those times were undercooked eggs and burnt hot dogs.

"FORGET IT!" I snapped, rushing down the stairs and into the kitchen. Grabbing a plastic bag from the cabinet, I started shoving graham crackers into it. I couldn't help but mumble to myself: *It's marvelous that husbands believe these items "magically" replenish themselves each week. It's as if they believe the Whole Foods fairy flies in their homes at night, gently placing sundries in their closets and groceries in their cabinets, leaving behind no traces of magical dust. I mean, Jesus; look for yourself every now and again. Is that so fucking hard?*

My thoughts were interrupted by my Aunt Lisa's car horn. She'd arrived to pick up Maya and West, taking them to school and her house, respectively. I naturally assumed I'd shed a thug tear if James left me, but I'd downright "slide-down-a-bathroom-door-R&B-music-video cry" if that older black woman ever left my life.

God, I was happy it was September. Summer was over, and these kids were out the door. But did that really even matter? Today was still a day like any other. I was there to help *all* my family start their own day on the right foot, but as usual, no one ever helped me with mine.

8:45 AM: Head to work! 📷

By the grace of God, the pussy-footing posse didn't make me late for the Acela Express from Baltimore to New York. I drove into the city, arriving at Baltimore's Penn Station before the iPhone alarm went off. My OCD loves when that happens.

I loved coming into the heart of the city, leaving my judgmental and uppity-ass neighborhood. It's ironic. I worked so hard to move into that colonial cage, and albeit giant, I missed living in downtown Baltimore with its diverse culture and authenticity.

Would you look at that, I pondered to myself. Other grownups- er, I mean ADULTS. Grownups is a kid word. I felt a release as I thought, look at all these adults just waiting to have adult conversations!

I was excited to return to society as Christine Michel Carter, the woman, and global communications strategist. I genuinely loved my job and my family equally, but I gotta tell ya, sometimes my traditional-colonial felt like a prison. My ankle bracelet malfunctioned at 8:45, and miraculously I could leave the house for ten hours to converse with grownups.

Dammit, ADULTS.

It wasn't uncommon for me to spend more time in Ubers or on Acela trains than in actual meetings. It also wasn't unusual for me to be in an entirely different state during business hours, and yet I still had to be home by six p.m., picking my kids up from Aunt Lisa's. Today was no different. I was headed to NYC to interview La La Anthony for an upcoming Forbes piece on the rise of female crowd funders.

I purchased my Amtrak ticket and headed to the platform. While waiting for the train, I decided to scroll Instagram. Someone had reposted a quote from Annabel Crabb:

The conundrum for working mothers is an exact one: the feeling that one ought to work as if one did not have children while raising one's children as if one did not have a job.

Tell me about it, I chuckled inside.

NYC was quickly becoming a home away from home. Between speaking at conferences and podcasts and TV interviews, I found myself making this commute every month! For today's trip, I decided to meet a personal goal: talk to one stranger for an hour. A feat easier said than done, as I usually liked to sit alone in first class. I could be found in a corner, knees facing the window, replying to Instagram comments on my page. Unbothered.

Not today, Carter. I boarded the train and shuffled side to side, moving to the first-class car. As I looked around, I saw open pairs of seats and pinched my arm to remind myself of my goal. I must sit with someone.

"Is this seat available?" I asked what appeared to be a forty-something white man, his slim frame decked out in an Express Men's finest suit.

"Please, sit down. I'm just reviewing some notes," he responded.

"Hi, I'm Christine." My voice cracked.

"Christine? Henry Reshin. Pleasure." He greeted me with a confident smirk.

Shit, this is hard.

"Henry, what's taking you to NYC?"

"I'm speaking to students at the Stern School of Business," he said. "Last year, I wrote a book on financial planning; you know, setting yourself up for success in the future. A friend of mine who's a professor at NYU asked me to speak to his class."

Damn, Henry. How many "I's" and "me's" can one fit into a sentence? No, Christine, no! I barked to myself as if I were a puppy. This man is NOT Trump; he did nothing to you. Don't judge a book by its cover.

It's my opinion that when one receives an advanced degree, the university also gives you an optional stick to put up your ass. From the looks and tone of Henry, he had decided to let his stick start paying rent up there.

I turned on my iPhone, and Henry glanced at my screen. @CNBC's Instagram post appeared—news about Facebook with a picture of Sheryl Sandberg.

"Oh, you're a fan of Sheryl Sandberg?" Henry asked.

"Nope," I replied a little too quickly for Henry's taste.

Dammit. Why couldn't he have seen a picture of Michael B. Jordan instead? He wouldn't have asked me questions about that. I explained why I answered abruptly:

> "I understand *Lean In* is heralded in the workforce community, but I sadly find it difficult to see myself in her experience. As a black millennial mother, I'm unable to 'lean in' with as much ease as she did—even with the high amount of visibility, I have to the leadership team at my company. And though I respect and applaud Sandberg for pushing the corporate feminist agenda, she was in a high-level, high-profile position and therefore could do so."

"She seems smart. You don't find her credible?" Henry questioned as if I was going against my own kind. Truth be told, Henry's arrogance made me feel he was gonna argue whatever point I made.

I responded:

> "Sandberg easily establishes credibility, but she isn't relatable. I'm trying to juggle the same aspects of my life as she was—parenting, career, and marriage—and I read her book in the hopes it would provide solace. But as a quadruple minority in my workplace, I just can't identify my experience in Sandberg's. When she started 'leaning in,' she was well into her thirties and serving as Google's vice president of global online sales and operations.

Before that, she was the chief of staff for United States Secretary of the Treasury Lawrence Summers!

Oop! Boo, you didn't know she was smart, did she? I giggled internally.

> "When one has those titles on their résumé, leaning in isn't the hardest thing ever. But try that when you're entry-level. She, of course, shouldn't apologize for going to Harvard, working in Silicon Valley, etc. But shit—I sure as hell didn't. If my black ass took her advice and 'leaned in,' the next place you'll find me leaning anywhere is over a counter at Burger King to clarify an order."

Dammit, Christine! Too ethnic too soon. Be woke, but don't be another angry black woman.

Eh, whatevs.

We switched facial expressions; his smile slid down his face and right up to mine. But the truth is that, unlike Henry and the Sheryl Sandbergs of corporate America, most of the time I was the only black person in the room. I was usually the primary target for ethnic and mansplaining. I always stuck out like a sore thumb.

What was it about the Henrys of the corporate world that made me feel like an impostor? After all, my résumé spoke for itself: I'd spent over a decade in marketing, supporting executive leaders at innovative, category-leading companies. I spoke at national conferences and regularly contributed to Forbes, covering working parents, millennial women, and black millennials.

I could write articles all day long for my readers; my tribe. But I had the receipts of men that looked like Henry commenting on pieces, calling me a "shit starter" and a "black bitch." Comments like that— no matter how confident I'd like to be—only exacerbated my impostor syndrome.

My cell phone rang.

"Excuse me, Henry; I have to take this." I swiped to answer the call. "This is Christine."

"I just got a text from CVS. Maya's prescription is ready. Can you pick it up?" James asked.

I turned to the train window, my back facing Henry. "James, I thought the purpose of you getting the texts was so you could help me out and pick up the prescription on your lunch break. You know I'm on a damn train to NYC!" I stealth-whispered into the phone.

"Never mind. I'll do it when I get back," I answered, smashing the red circle with my pointer finger. Why he doesn't have the time to run errands, but somehow, it's fair for me to do them, I'll never understand. He needs to figure out how to do it during or after work to just like I do!

8:00 PM: Dinner on the table! 🍴

My chances of stress eating were never higher than when I came home after a workday. Every evening, I struggled to figure out what to cook for dinner after I had already raced around the beltway, picking up my kids. I cooked from Sunday to Thursday, but each night I pondered: *What did I buy this week that James and the kids will be in the mood for? What awful shit did I eat last night that I now need to counterbalance? How long will it take to cook?* And on and on and on.

Tonight, I simply gave up, yelling, *Fuck it!* I took the kids to Chick-Fil-A.

Sure was gonna miss my nighttime glass of wine, though. That was the one problem with Chick-Fil-A. If they figured that shit out, they could have all the coins. Being a working mother of two taught me I CAN do all things through Christ, but I MUST do all things with the help of Sutter Home. In short, when it came to dinner, I was a huge fan of having a glass of wine during—

scratch that, after—

scratch that, before—

Fuck it. I was a huge fan of having a glass of wine anytime during the evening meal experience. I *tried* to keep a healthy diet, which included watching my alcohol intake. After all, I know the facts: women who drink in moderation are less likely than non-drinkers to be obese. But I'm pretty sure I didn't drink moderately. In fact, I was once asked by a doctor if I drink rarely, moderately, or heavily.

"Parentally," I replied.

The funny thing is, though not a real answer, he understood just what I meant. Parentally drinking is the fine line between moderately and heavily. And I didn't plan on stopping anytime soon. Why? Two reasons: 1.) That freaking beverage tasted delicious, and 2.) I had three kids, who were five, two, and 31 years old.

Kudos to the mothers who clutched their pearls, waving their paper fans while saying, "Oh, I detest mothers who drink, and drink around their children at that. Vile!"

Bitch, not only did my kids KNOW I drank; they knew it made Mommy a little less Betty Draper and a little more Betty Crocker. Maya could point out what "Mom juice" looked like in a kitchen cabinet, but she wasn't stupid. When I once asked her, fully relaxed from a glass of cabernet sauvignon, "Do you know what Mom juice actually is?" Maya replied, "Of course, Mommy. It's alcohol."

Parking the truck at Chick-fil-A, I got everyone out of their car seats (all the while sarcastically begging them to move at a more glacial pace like Miranda Priestly). Suddenly, I heard:

"Chrissy?"

It was my friend Melanie! A FRIEND! I saw a friend during the work week! Do you know how rare that was? Well, not really. It seemed like moms always saw friends across the aisle in a grocery store picking up applesauce, as opposed to across the booth in a bar drinking Old Fashioneds. Still, I considered this divine intervention and asked:

"Heyyyy, Melanie! What are you doing? Picking up dinner for you and Cara?"

Cara was Melanie's well-behaved daughter with her husband, Kevin. She always used manners when asking for ketchup to accompany her chicken nuggets. She was the exact opposite of my children. In fact, Maya was the Bizzaro to her Superman daughter.

"Yeah, just me and Cara," she replied. "We just went to see the latest Avengers movie. Have you seen it yet?"

"Naw." At the beginning of motherhood, I tried to hold on for cool points when people asked, 'Have you heard that new rap group?' or 'Have you seen that new movie?' Still, the time had passed and snowballed so quickly. I hadn't ever heard albums from some of my favorite artists or seen movies well into their sequels.

Melanie leaned in, lowering her voice so Maya and West couldn't hear. "You know I separated from Kevin, right? A few weeks ago."

In a second, my mind raced with negative thoughts, wondering how broken her family was going to be without both parents in the household. Wondering how long it would take for Cara to turn from a respectable, polite young girl to a spoiled terror. I was shocked.

"NO, I HADN'T," I exclaimed, a little too loud. I felt like a self-involved, horrible friend. As she explained the course of events that lead to her separation from her husband of eight years, I tilted my head to the side and nodded in agreement. Somehow, the whines of my children asking to go inside to eat were stifled. All that existed at that moment was Melanie and me.

"We just weren't connecting anymore, you know? We drifted apart. I don't know. Maybe it was because we got married too young or had a child too soon, but it just became clear that I was the doormat of the house. Unappreciated. I was miserable every morning and..."

I worried to myself...*that sounds familiar!* But I maintained my concerned expression and listened.

"The biggest sign was that I was confiding and sharing my feelings with someone other than Kevin. It was giving me that feeling of being appreciated, accepted, and just like... acknowledged, you know? I was a human again, instead of just a mom and wife. But later, I learned in couples counseling that it was no different than an affair."

I groaned, "I'm so sorry to hear that, Mel. I know motherhood and marriage aren't always easy..." I blanked, having zero idea what to say next. *Shit. What should I say to offer comfort?*

"I mean..." I shrugged. "I constantly read articles about other wives and mothers who've experienced the same thing you're going through. No one's perfect. Life isn't pleasant all the time, but striving for it will pay off in the end."

Melanie looked at me, puzzled, tilting her head as she closed her eyes, sighed, and smiled. *Shit. Did I say something wrong? Could she see through me?* I was usually THE pillar of support for everyone around me. I was the woman with the answers.

"Did you need any help with the kids in there? Just you? Where's James?" Melanie asked.

*Uuuhhhh...*I decided to quickly cut the awkward tension with my built-in diversion—my badass kids.

"No, I'm good. Listen, honey, I gotta get Maya and West their dinner. I'll call you a little bit later, okay?"

With that, Melanie hugged me goodbye.

10:00 PM: You need eight hours. Take your ass to sleep!

Night peeing was the best.

Unfortunately, when you're as much of a fan of controlling every aspect of your life as I was (my iPhone home and lock screens were my daily gym routine and caloric intake), necessary human acts that fluctuate throughout the day—such as peeing—often go ignored. Sometimes I didn't pee for hours when I was in the zone, writing a presentation.

Enter the self-care moment that was "night peeing;" my one moment of privacy. Night peeing was the act of using the bathroom entirely in the dark, so that no one knew I was in it. I usually brought my phone (oh so sanitary, I know), scrolling "black hair braids for work" on Pinterest.

This particular night, I was found out. Mid-piss, I looked up and found an eerie three-foot figure standing in the doorway with his feet apart. He breathed heavily, staring at me like Michael Myers in *Halloween.*

"Yes, West?" I asked. Can I unwind for a MINUTE?!

"Tukmein," he demanded. As if I didn't tuck him in hours ago.

"Okay, one second. Where's Daddy?"

"YOU! You Tukmein!" he grunted again.

God forbid you disturb your father. James could rest but me...I hadn't gotten a full night of sleep since Barack Obama's first term as president. Because that's when I didn't have kids. I could charge money to watch James sleep at night; he slept so comfortably. And after more than a decade together, the man still hadn't learned how to share a bed. He grunted, snorted, and swung more limbs at me as he slept than a male gorilla. Then, he actually had the *nerve* to be irritated and hurt when I asked him to stick to his side of the bed! Every night he sweated so atrociously the pillows smelled like dirty nickels. Even with sheet-suspenders on the bed, I could never keep covers on my side. His limb swinging snapped them off the sheets when he rolled himself up like a cozy, massive Twinkie.

"I'll be in your room in a minute," I scream-whispered to West, a hidden talent that came with motherhood. West stared at me for a minute before walking off and leaving the door wide open behind him. I dropped my head to my knees.

I sang to myself,

> *"This is the job that never ends. Yes, it goes on and on, my friend. Some people started having kids, not knowing what it does, and they'll continue having kids forever just because..."*

I chuckled. My world was pure chaos. A fucking mess. It was funny to think about the single people who believed getting married and having kids meant doing the same thing day in and day out." HA! I WISH that shit were true. Between last-minute grocery store trips for chicken nuggets, emergency "West has an ear infection" calls from Aunt Lisa, and unexpected evening work events—my weeks became unpredictable AFTER I got married and had kids!

But that night, I couldn't get Melanie's expression (after my half-ass words of comfort) out of my mind. What made my life so different from hers? I was an exhausted professional, wife, and mother to TWO kids. Every day I busted into rooms *just* in time—not one minute early—like Kramer into Jerry Seinfeld's apartment. Hell, I always drove twenty miles over the speed limit, just to get from point A to point B. But still, I was late once or twice a week.

Maintaining this amount of energy to do everything I needed to do (with erratic but necessary bursts on top of *that*) was exhausting. I doubted that I was doing an excellent job at motherhood, and yet I doubted I would ever say I needed help.

I am a woman with no control, I admitted to myself. I wanted the freedom to choose whether I wanted to play dress-up with my daughter or get a massage. (Sure, I'd probably choose to get the massage, but the minute I got to the spa, I'd just FaceTime Maya and ask her "What you doing?")

I was killing myself so that others could live. Sacrificing everything.

I felt like Jesus Carter.

I wished the Whole Foods fairy DID exist. I wished there were someone who could help me with managing my life, my career, my children, and myself. Someone who could handle the ridiculous moments, like cleaning the bathroom floor after West peed on it right before hopping into the bath. Or, moments when I was impatiently

waiting behind the woman at Target, who was compelled to argue about a ten-percent-off coupon's expiration date.

But...isn't all that what a husband is supposed to do? I questioned.

In the middle of scrolling, a text message appeared on my screen:

"U up?"

I deleted it and kept singing to myself.

I was killing myself so that others could live. Sacrificing everything.

I felt like Jesus Carter.

Chapter Two

What A Difference Six F***ing Inches Make

"All I got is...ain't got no time, just burning daylight, still love, and...and it's still love..."

I parked at the open spot in front of the restaurant, unapologetically blasting SZA and singing off-key at the top of my lungs. Guests waiting for the cars from the valet scoffed, giving me side-eye and all-around *don't-you-have-any-home-training?* looks.

"Nope, I sure don't," I expressed back to them in a stare, my head tilted and lips pursed.

I spotted James, already parked and waiting for me. Smiling at one another, I walked up to him. "How are you?" he asked.

"I'm well. Let's do this."

I leaned into his body, my head inches from his chest. I pulled his jacket tighter so he wouldn't catch a cold from the brisk October weather. For a brief moment, we locked eyes.

"Your neck is getting a rash. Are you overeating dairy because your eczema is flaring up." I scolded, "I'll give you some coconut oil to put on it when we get in the house."

James stared at me as if I missed a social cue. Then, stepping back, he waved his arm for me to pass into the restaurant.

I opened the door with James behind me, and we went inside to meet our dinner guests. This meal was part pleasure, part business. I'd asked a family friend and older colleague of mine, Shaun, if he and his wife Sheila wouldn't mind being interviewed for an upcoming article I was writing for *Health* magazine. The article was becoming data-heavy and needed a personal perspective. It could benefit from marital tips from a couple with children who'd been married for decades.

Usually, I'm skeptical about interviewing older married couples because society suggests (and thus, the older married couples believe) that their age makes them well equipped to provide advice. In my opinion, just because great-aunt-and-uncle-so-and-so were married for 50 years doesn't mean they are equipped to dish out marital advice. Many of them are secretly living postmodern era marriages: financial and/or familial contracts that have nothing to do with love and personal fulfillment. Older generations can't always comprehend (much less provide an example of) what it means to be newlyweds in today's society. That's like asking someone still using a typewriter how to jailbreak your iPhone.

Finding a couple to interview was also not as easy a feat as one would think. Fifteen percent of new parents are divorced three years after they welcome their first child into the world. And if they manage to stay married and raise children, even more divorce occurs the moment their children graduate high school. Seriously. Everybody thinks older married couples are committed, experienced, and wiser, but "gray divorce"—divorce among U.S. adults ages 50 and older—is on the rise. In 2015, for every 1,000 married persons ages 50 and older, ten divorced—up from five in 1990.

But Shaun and Sheila were different. I loved their relationship story, mainly how Shaun supported Sheila's decision to become a working mom. When they first got married 30 years ago, Sheila went from waiting tables to managing restaurants to an office job in the financial services industry at Alex Brown. Twenty years later, she is now T. Rowe Price's top national salesperson. They viewed each chapter of their lives together as just one in a book of many. They never knew what was next around the corner, and for them, that was cool. Their only plan was to continue supporting each other as they made choices along the way.

We spotted Shaun and Sheila at the bar, where they were fully engaged in a conversation with one another, patiently waiting for us to arrive. I noticed how Shaun looked at Sheila as she spoke, turning his entire body on the stool to face her, smiling and nodding as she talked. It was as if he couldn't wait to hear what this intelligent woman had to say. Sheila's body was turned as well, and as she spoke, she made gestures and funny faces that that made Shaun laugh. Their glasses of merlot were still full. They were so engulfed in one another that they didn't even notice the bartender had delivered them.

Meanwhile, I can't even get a damn door opened for me. I shook my head, forcing an attitude adjustment.

"Hiiii, guys!"

Shaun and Sheila slowly broke their stare at one another and turned. "Heyyyy!!!!!"

We all hugged one another, and as the hostess came over. "Your table is ready."

Shaun, Sheila, James, and I headed to our table. It didn't take us long to order drinks, an appetizer for the table, and our dinner. After a bit of small talk and personal conversation, our appetizers arrived—calamari, seared ahi tuna, and mini Maryland crab cakes. I put my iPhone on the table so I could start recording our conversation. Like Tiffany Haddish, #SheReady to work.

"So Shaunnnn and Sheilayyy," I sang their names. "Thanks again for agreeing to be interviewed. You've been married 30 years, with children at that! I think it's important for *Health* readers to hear the good, bad, and ugly of your story."

"Of course," Sheila replied. She had such a warm, bubbly spirit that kept her looking youthful in her fifties. "Hit us with the first question."

"What was the best marital advice you received before you walked down the aisle?"

Shaun replied with his firm, commanding voice, "It was third party advice. The cantor that married us interviews every couple he marries before the actual ceremony. He told us that one couple wrote their vows to read that they would love each other 'until death do us part or until our love dies.' Their thought was that should one of them should stop loving the other for any reason, they loved each other now so much that they wanted to commit to letting that person go."

I didn't even need to look at James. His silence told me he was making the same facial expression as me. We'd mastered grinning and nodding when we heard relationship advice from older couples, but on the inside, we mocked, "What a crock of shit."

"Do your parents or in-laws give you marital advice? What is their role in your marriage?" I asked.

Sheila chose to answer this one: "Shaun and I always roll together when spending time with parents, spending holidays with as many family members as possible. But when our parents are putting pressure on us, Shaun and I are the "family" that matters first. We look at "pressure" as being on us (as a unit), not one partner or the other. We handle our own stuff and don't talk with parents about the problems of our relationship. That's part of what being married means."

Damn, shit must be nice, I responded in my mind. My mind drifted to a conversation my father-in-law once had with James.

"Christine is not a traditional South Carolina housewife," he remarked to his son in a discouraging tone. He meant that Southern black wives were better at matrimony. I was destined to be a disappointment because I wasn't traditional. When Handsome McHandsomekins told me this, I laughed. I'm a Maryland—no, excuse me—a Baltimore wife, honey. You are a lucky man! Plus, considering the so-called traditional South Carolina housewife that my monster-in-law is? Well, let's just say I questioned where any advice from that long, committed marriage came from.

I guess it's great that in this 21st century of ours, so many young wives made best friends out of their mothers-in-law. But I was the young wife bringing back hating her mother-in-law. Like, really committed *Game of Thrones* hating. And I was unashamed to say it.

"Sheila," I interrupted my own train of thought. "As a top sales executive and all-around badass mother, how do you handle the household finances?"

Sheila replied confidently, "We absolutely agree to have full financial disclosure about each of our personal financial situations at all times," she shrugged. "We don't make any substantial purchases without consulting each other first. In the early years, things were thinner. Still, our plan was simple: don't spend more than we have, live within our means, and save as often as we can. We now have a financial planner but have always made it a point to live within our means. Our son Michael is now a sophomore in college and has never once asked us for money."

"That's impressive," I noted with a mouthful of tuna.

"You know Chrissy and I met in college," James pointed out. "I never once asked my parents for money...but for VERY different reasons!" We both laughed at the shade he brought to the conversation.

Shaun didn't catch it. "Why?" he asked.

"They didn't have any!" James joked.

The waiter was clearing our appetizers, as dinner arrived. "Guys, I think I've got enough here. Thank you so much! Let's just eat!"

"Of course!" they responded in unison.

Jesus; this fucking couple. They're friends, so they're easy to love. But they're in love, so they're easy to hate.

"I think people will honestly appreciate your perspective and..."

James interrupted, "Can I ask a question to both of you? I'm curious if your parents were, or are, still married."

"Mine aren't," Shaun noted. "My mom and dad were divorced when I was seven. I grew up with my mom. She always had my back and was my best friend. She brought no vices to the table, so it was easy to follow her example. She also loved to have fun and still does."

"I had a very different upbringing," Sheila admitted while looking at her sea bass. "My parents were married, but my dad died quite suddenly when I was 18. I learned how to be frugal and respect the value of money from my mom, and I have passed that on to Michael."

Sheila's voice trailed off. It was the first time I heard her voice in a lower tone. Shaun interjected as though he was protecting her.

"Sheila shows Michael the love and care that she never had growing up."

I knew where James was headed with his question, and I could see him summarizing their answers in his head. *So one momma's boy and the other raised by both parents, until tragedy struck.* James clearly picked up on the romantic cues they'd been giving all night. But, I don't know if it was my question about in-laws or the one about money that made him ask about their parents' marriages.

Perhaps he was trying to learn how one's upbringing affected their marriage and how they parent. Over three decades, his parents had been separated three times. I'm no marriage therapist, but those two people should not be married. When I dated James in college, he'd have to come to my house to study on the weekends. He couldn't concentrate at home, with the two of them fighting for 48 hours straight.

To this day, he's awkwardly and inappropriately spoiled by his mother, and it affected our marriage. James' father worked long, irregular hours, so my monster-in-law replaced him with her son. He's an only child suffering from black momma syndrome: the act of raising one's son in the hopes he'll grow to take on the financial and emotional responsibilities of a spouse. For generations, it's been a common practice among black women, and to this day, there is no cure.

On the flip side of that, I came from a divorced household; my parents divorced when I was nine months old. I didn't know what it was like to have my mother and father in the same house, but from their heated joint encounters with me at school events and birthday parties, I knew I didn't wanna know, either!

A half-hour passed. Shaun and James argued over who would pay for dinner, and I won. I slowly pulled my credit card from my wallet. The waiter nearly snatched it from my cold, frugal hands, and I paid the check. We said our goodbyes, thankful for the opportunity to have learned something new about one another.

James walked me to my car, and once again, we locked eyes as we stood no more than six inches away from each other.

"Alright, I'll see you back at the house," he said.

With that, we stepped out of each other's paths and walked to our respective trucks. I hopped in and immediately checked my phone: six emails and one missed text message. Looking up in exhaustion and through the passenger window, I saw Shaun and Sheila standing next to their car. They stood no more than six inches away from one another. Sheila leaned into Shaun's body, and the two were locked in a stare. She tilted her head up, and they kissed.

"ARGGGHHHH!!! UGH!" I yelled, looking up at the car ceiling. I exhaled, put the phone back in my purse, and started the engine.

"It's still love, still love (still lovin'), still love," I lip-sync, "It's still love, but it's still love..."

Over the next four days, I helped Maya recover from an adenotonsillectomy. The shit seems as painful to recover from as it is to say, but basically, it was an operation to remove both her adenoids and tonsils. I worked from home and taped podcast interviews during the evening in an attempt to not miss a beat.

Maya was in so much pain during the day from her sore throat. By day three, I'd decided to stop sleeping through the night in the event she needed me then too. I was used to not getting eight hours of sleep. I tend to train my body to deal without it since on the off occasion I did hit REM, I'd always have to spring up from that slumber anyway. It was not so easy.

It will get better one day. For now, you gotta keep these people safe, I hoped.

This surgery recovery was becoming my own personal war story. By day three, I started journaling. On day four, I wrote:

DAY 4. Coffee is all that keeps me going. I mean, I say this with the utmost respect but stay-at-home moms...how? Just...how? #SAHM #howdoyoudoit #keepyaheadup #respect

Stay-at-home moms deserve ALL the coins, ALL the glory, and ALL the credit. They are undoubtedly fucking doing God's work over here.

Let's see. What was driving me the craziest? Was it Maya's reliance on her iPad to get through the day? She was watching Charli's Crafty Kitchen for hours, occasionally pausing the YouTube video to demand Siri tell her how to spell a word. (I can't lie, though;

sometimes I do reap the benefits of her iPad devotion. I'm guilty of sending her pins of cute hairstyles myself.)

Was it all the questions, as if every day is "ask-a-million-questions" day and she needs to celebrate in a big, big way?

Or was it the absence of dialogue between me and another adult?

No. It was none of them. It had to be ignoring me for eight hours.

I peeked my head into the family room and only saw a brown puffball behind a hot pink, shockproof iPad cover.

"If you like what you've seen, don't forget to subscribe to my YouTube channel, or like and comment below."

WTF? This child didn't even have an email address, let alone a YouTube channel. What was Miss Bossy talking about?

"Maya. Maya. *Maya*. Maya. MAYA!" I screamed.

"YES, Mommy." she barely groaned, back on the arm of the sectional, legs propped up by a pillow, and covered by a blanket.

I honestly believed she wasn't that sick. At that point, recovery was near complete, but Maya, the sharp fox, was born an actress. She was born nine weeks early, screaming at the top of her lungs, and her resting heart rate in the NICU was the rate of a full-term baby. She had always commanded attention, and for her, this recovery was her opportunity to earn a Best Actress nod from the Academy.

"Did you ask your father for medicines before he left for work?"

"He said to ask you for it." She gave me a look to imply she needed privacy and wanted me to leave. Girl ain't even got a credit score. Looking at me like she's a woman. *Hmph.*

Well, what the fuck? I'm the one that took off work all this week to deal with this. The least your ass coulda did was....

Just then, Maya stopped me in my tracks and asked, "When I feel better, can you make me some strawberry pancakes and sausages?"

"We don't have any," I grumbled.

"Well, why not?"

How Sway? When was I gonna get that shit? I thought. I'm trapped in this house just like you!

"Mommy, are you happy as a balloon, or are you doomed?"

Maya disarmed me. I honestly didn't have an answer for it.

I continued collecting the popsicle wrappers from the coffee table and left the room. As I walked into the kitchen, I pulled Maya's artwork off the fridge—throwing it in the trash can with the popsicle wrappers. Instantly, I felt calm.

Later that evening, I was thrilled when I heard three beeps from our alarm system. It meant her father was home. It was time to change shifts! I didn't know who was happier to be free from madness, me or the man at the end of *Cabin Fever,* who realized he was the only one who made it without being infected. I mean, I, too, was raising my arms in victory while shouting *YES!* as that alarm went off.

"Hi!" I exclaimed, rushing to the back door to greet him. "Did you pick up her prescriptions?" Kissing him at first sight was the last thing I was thinking about doing. I wanted the drugs.

"No, I figured you'd do it. You had the prescription card," James replied.

WHAT?!

"JESUS! MUST I DO EVERYTHING!" I barked. I stared at his face and could see his exhaustion. I didn't know if it was from working all day or if it was from me.

"Let me help," he pleaded. "I'll go back out and pick them up."

"NO!" I snapped. "At this point, I'll just go get them myself. I have the prescription card, after all, right?" The bitch in me was loose. Katie had gone kaboom. "I made your dinner and left it on the stove for you. It's fried catfish and mashed potatoes."

"I'm not hungry," he insisted in a whisper under his breath. From the corner of my eye, I saw Maya coming into the kitchen to hug her father. I quickly adjusted my facial expression from pissed to pleasant.

"Hi Daddy," she whimpered, one hand on her forehead and the other on her stomach. "I'm feeling a bit better today. Were you and Mommy fussing?"

"Noooooo," we said in unison, fake grins plastered on our faces. "I don't know what you thought you heard, but we weren't arguing," I added. James brushed past me and headed to the basement.

We agreed the kids don't need to hear us arguing or see us bickering with one another. He'd had enough of that as a child, and he didn't want it for Maya and West too.

"Why are you guys up at 7am on a Saturday? You kids are driving me CRAZY!" I whispered, looking at the two big-eyed creatures staring at me from my bedside.

"That's because we want you crazy," Maya boasted. "And we're hungry."

What the fuck? I thought. *Can't make this stuff up if I tried.* Raising kids could be an entire Alanis Morissette song.

"It's like finally washing your bedsheets, and the kids vomit on them instead of their own when they're sick. It's like kids waking up at 7 a.m. on Saturday, and 10 a.m. on Tuesday."

I'd made it to the weekend but made my goal was to finalize where West would start daycare next month. A few hours later, I called my top daycare choice, Mystery Pals, asking the owner follow-up questions.

Chapter Two
What A Difference Six F***ing Inches Make

"Good morning," I sang. "May I speak with Tonya, please?"

I heard a slight groan. "This is her. Good morning, Mrs. Carter."

These people better get their life, I thought. *They don't seem to mind taking my money with a hello and a smile.* "Thanks for taking my call on a Saturday. I just wanted to ask a few more questions regarding the Mystery Pals Daycare. What holidays and other days is the facility closed? In the event of a weather emergency, do you follow Baltimore City or Baltimore County school closings? Are you NAEYC accredited? Are background checks conducted on all staff members? Do you feel comfortable administering medi—"

She interjected, and I heard rustling papers on the other end. "Mrs. Carter, give me a moment to write down your questions. I want to make sure to answer them all."

If you thought Maya needed the utmost medical attention, honey, she ain't got shit on my little bear cub West. He, too, takes a liquid and nasal allergy medication and vitamins every day, but his meals have to be considered days in advance, as he's lactose-intolerant and has an egg allergy.

My Oedipus West. I didn't realize I'd be one of those moms who quacked like a duck to clip a boy's toenails but, here we are. We both have the same big eyes, animated expressions, and eat healthy foods like teff and dried barberries. I'd slow danced to Sade with him barefoot in the kitchen at least 20 times; with his father: two. West has better rhythm.

Now that we were hitting a milestone together with him starting daycare, I was a bit broken-hearted. I wasn't prepared for dealing with another child's social calendar: school birthday parties, sleepovers... uggggghhhh!!! (Let me tell you there are some things God created, and some things that the devil created. Having to attend your child's schoolmate's birthday party or talking to people you don't even want to know for more than one minute during pick up and drop off... that's something the devil created.)

But West is a different breed, and let's call a spade a spade. He's a black boy born in Baltimore. He lives comfortably, but his exterior still presents him as a public enemy. When I lay softly on his chest, I'm unsettlingly aware of his heartbeat; his mortality. I don't let him run in our backyard or pretend to play with toy guns. I thought of Maya as a preemie when I watched the sleeping babies in the Pampers holiday commercial, but as West sleeps on his back with his hands above his head, all I think is, *stop shooting us.*

I've got a bit of post-traumatic stress disorder from seeing so many black men killed by the police, especially those killings that occur in my city—like Freddie Gray. I internalized every news segment, thinking *that was someone's West. Someone's son. What makes my son any safer?*

I'm responsible for multiple lives. I take that fact very seriously. Perhaps too seriously.

My persistent worry caused me to lose focus on the conversation with Tonya. James walked into the kitchen, listening to the end of my phone call. He'd just woken up because he's entitled to enjoy his weekend slumber. #puresarcasm

"You know, your son is gonna have his little thotties. He's gonna leave the nest and find someone. All we're doing today is finding him a daycare. You don't have to be so hard on the woman." West wandered into the kitchen, brushing past his father to hand me a juice box to open.

"Thank you, James," I proclaimed, hitting defense mode. "I'm aware of that fact." West rubbed my thigh. I moved his hand. "West, please don't rub Mommy that way." I picked up West, plopping him on the counter while I opened the juice box.

James scoffed, "So why do you have to be so uptight about it? Why does everything have to go your way?"

"I know I put a lot of love into the kids," I responded in a serious tone. "But *they* haven't hurt me like some others have, so why should I hurt them?"

I kissed Oedipus West on the forehead and stood him on the floor. He flashed those big eyes at me as he drank his apple juice.

I'm responsible for multiple lives. I take that fact very seriously.

Perhaps too seriously.

CHAPTER THREE

MY DAUGHTER F***ING ROCKS, THANK YOU VERY MUCH

"You, my dear, took a vow. And when things didn't go your way, you simply broke that vow. I come from a generation of women that valued marriage. We believed in 'for better or for worse.' Not 'for better, or until the road gets rocky.' When I think of the heartache and shame, you caused my dear boy... I'm amazed that you could even come here and look me in the face."

Charlotte couldn't fight anymore. It seemed to her she'd been fighting for this marriage forever.

W*hat a bitch*, I snapped. Reminded me of someone in my life. I truly hated Bunny MacDougal. Back in 2002, when this episode of "Sex and the City" initially aired, I thought there couldn't be a mother-in-law worse than her.

"Mommy, are you ready?" Maya asked.

Thanks for derailing THAT awful train, Maya. "Yup, let's do it. Come here and sit between my legs."

Today was the annual Christmas pageant at Maya's school, and this was the last year she'd participate. Second graders just aren't adorable enough to perform holiday carols for a gymnasium full of parents.

To save $60 on a wash and two-strand twists at the hairdresser, I was attempting to do Maya's hair myself. We'd just decided on a style after I searched "black girl hair" on Pinterest. She wanted something that would show off her natural hair, and I loved that idea. Maya was one of three black girls in the entire class of 30 students. I loved it whenever she chose to accent vital moments in her "kid world" with natural hair.

I reluctantly turned the TV from "Sex and the City" to the Disney channel.

"Oh look, *Descendants 2* is on for the 80th time," I whined.

"Yes, and we will watch it." Maya ignored my sarcasm. Gotta give it to her. The kid's got chutzpah.

7:00 a.m. Thirty minutes before we have to walk out the door- and I was just starting this kid's hair? And a *new* style at that? What the hell was I thinking? Tapping on the image, I was redirected to the hairstyle's link with wikiHow instructions on how to do complete the two-strand twists:

> *Two-strand twists are a versatile hairstyle that can work on either short or long hair. The necessary two-strand twists can be used as a base hairstyle for many different variations so that each hairdresser can give an individualized look. Children can also benefit from this easy-to-keep hairstyle since it can be dressed up with ribbons or beads. Follow the steps below to learn how to do two-strand twists with a professional look that can be another added hairstyle choice for your hair care routine.*

Blah blah blah. I scrolled up to scan the article for the images that looked closest to Maya's current hair state. Then, I blow-dried and cleaned her curly hair.

"Mommy, where's my juice cup? Did you throw it away?" I heard West calling me from the kitchen on a footstool. How did I know he was on a stool? Mom radar. His voice was echoing at a higher level in the kitchen than usual. I knew my son didn't grow two feet overnight.

I jumped from the couch and rushed to the kitchen, nearly stepping on Maya in the process.

"GET DOWN! GET! DOWN! I will get your cup. JAMES! Can you please watch West while I do Maya's hair?" I yelled, grabbing West's cup from the fridge.

I heard their father standing up from the couch in the basement, shuffling up the stairs to get West. "Come here, man," he responded calmly. "What do you need?"

"Juice," I answered instead, "and I already grabbed it." I quickly handed James a glass of orange juice, heading back to the family room to finish Maya's hair.

Shit! My screen locked. Where was I?

While I tried to find where I'd stopped reading, my eyes caught an essential section on the page.

> *Once you have finished washing your hair, begin drying by only removing excess water...*

The next line stole my soul. I gasped.

> *It is very important to leave the hair a little damp.*

"FUCK! No, no, no, no, no, no, no! Crap!" I yelled. My cursing was so loud that I heard James running from the kitchen into the family room. "What's wrong?"

I had one job. I just assumed you needed to have fresh, clean, blow-dried hair for the style. I didn't know. But I'm a black woman, I should have KNOWN this. Ugh! I should have paid attention. I just wanted Maya to look perfect and pretty for her recital. I wanted to give her the one thing she asked me for, which was a killer hairstyle. I couldn't even do that right. Idiot.

My heart started racing, and I was finding it difficult to breathe. My chest felt tight. I fell to the couch and looked up at James. My eyes were wet, but tears weren't falling.

Handsome McHandsomekins rushed to my side with concern. "What? What?!"

"I can't do it," I whispered. "I tried...to..."

I felt chills spreading from my stomach, up to my back and into my arms and hands. In a matter of moments, I'd exhausted myself. I made myself physically tired because of my emotions.

"Are you hurt?" James questioned me sternly. I barely found the strength to shake my head and started clenching my fists.

He'd seen this behavior before. "You're having an anx—"

Maya and West were both in the family room, staring at their crippled mother with concern and confusion. *Get yourself together, got dammit. Don't be a punk*, I thought.

Do NOT let these kids see you like this.

I pursed my lips, shook my head to the side, and smiled.

"Sorry, guys," I interrupted. "Mommy was sad for a minute, but I'm fine now. Maya, I'm so sorry, baby, but I forgot a step in the directions. We don't have time for me to fix it, so I'm gonna give you hair like..."

I glanced up at the TV and saw *The Descendants*.

"Mal. I'm going to do your hair like Mal instead. AND, after school, we'll get some ice cream!"

"YAAAAYYY!!!" Maya screamed. "Great!"

"Before you jump back into that, do you need a minute to..." James stared at me. I shot him a look to beg him not to question my erratic behavior. I can't bring myself to address it right now.

"I'm fine."

James turned his gaze away from me and to the window, mumbling, "Alright."

We arrived at the elementary school and headed to the gymnasium. I'd slipped the first-grade teacher a $25 Starbucks gift card as her Christmas present, which secured me reserved front row seats to the pageant. Schools are like prisons, but both teachers and parents are inmates. Currency is not money—it's gift cards, early undocumented dismissals, classroom supplies, and today, front row seats.

Upon arriving at the reserved seats, I saw the teacher, Mrs. Thurman, talking with my own ray of sunshine—my mother-in-law, Bunny MacDougal. I guess she'd found no time to spray some water on herself this morning and run a comb through her raggedy ass wig. Still, she found more than enough time to smoke a Salem cigarette. I could smell her breath nine feet away.

Mrs. Thurman had a distressed look on her face, as though she'd been having an exchange with the Wicked Witch of West Baltimore.

"Hi, Christine, your mother..."

"Mother-in-law," I quickly responded.

"She arrived early, so I was just letting her know I marked these seats for your family."

"Thank you, Mrs. Thurman. We're here, and my parents each texted me that they'll be here shortly."

There we were: me, James, West, my father-in-law, and Hagatha. My parents would be there soon to keep the uncomfortable party going. I sat West to my right and James to my left. I gave zero fucks about where the other two sat. They're lucky I reserved seating.

Not a moment too early, my parents arrived at the same time, sitting in the last two reserved seats.

"Hi, Ma. Did you come here with my father?" I worried.

"Oh god no," she sassed, her eyes rolling at the mere thought of joint travel with him.

I wondered if the leftover resentment she had for my father made her unable to tell the two of us apart. We were once close—when I was five—before life drove us apart.

Her opinion of me today shouldn't concern me, but it does. She's still my mother. Yet I can't criticize *her*. Or expect an apology from *her*. I have to accept her for who she is, but not expect the same in return, which is complete bullshit.

I couldn't even lean over to whisper hello to my father before the show began. Maya and her class were already talking to the middle of the gymnasium floor, and I hollered. Maya walked from the back of the line to the center of the group, and I gasped.

"YES, BABY! Wooooooo!" I screamed before Maya even opened up her mouth to sing. She was commanding the audience. While her other classmates had on casual clothing, I'd dressed Maya that morning in a blue sequin gown with a large tulle petticoat. She stuck out like a sore thumb but shoot me. I wanted my daughter to shine bright like the diamond she is.

"That's our baby," I turned my head and beamed towards Handsome McHandsomekins. Sometimes I can't believe we're so lucky to have such incredible kids who are so confident and comfortable with themselves. I realized I might be doing this parenting shit right.

My own pat on the pack was premature, as, from the corner of my eye, I saw my mother-in-law tilt to James. She said in a not-so-subtle whisper with her gravely, chain-smoking voice, "Did *she* do her hair or was it professionally done? Next time I'll pay for Maya's hair to be done. I can see her split ends from here."

My chest got tight again. This time it was as if I was punched outside in the dead of winter. I could feel that blow. But no, I was not going to grant this bitch the satisfaction today. I clenched my jaw, breathing loudly enough to signal to James that "I heard what that heffa said, and you better address it." I kept smiling at Maya.

No, you know what? I thought, I'm not a bigger bitch. I'm the biggest bitch. And I know this bitch did NOT just try to sneak come for me.

I leaned over and turned my head, catching my mom's (and everyone else's) attention. I said to her—loudly so everyone could hear, of course—

"Maya's hair looks so amazing today, doesn't it? She's gorgeous! Thank God. It could have been SOOOOO much worse!"

I leaned back and sat up proud as a peacock. James whispered, "Really? Was that necessary?"

"Why yes, yes it was. Thanks for asking. Perhaps instead of scolding me, you should scold Darth Mother next to you." I smirked.

The first-grade class proceeded to take the audience through their renditions of *Christmas is Here, Feliz Navidad and Sleigh Bells.* Each song was louder but more incomprehensible than the last. Mrs.

Chapter Three
My Daughter F***ing Rocks, Thank You Very Much

Thurman's class finished their pageant, and the parents herded like cats from the gymnasium to the classroom. As we walked, James gives me a scolding in the hallway.

"Why? Why do you start with her? I ignore it. I'm not worried about her comments."

I angrily whisper-replied, "Because it's fucking annoying! Like, shut your got damn mouth!"

A parent in front of me turned his head to the right, and I could see his furrowed brow. He looked at me as if to say, "Watch your mouth. You're cursing in a school."

I bugged my eyes back, as if to say, "You can get it too. ANYBODY can get it in this bitch right now." He turned around and kept walking.

"Her hair looked fine," he added.

"It's not about her hair!" I snapped. "I do a lot. Like A LOT. I'm trying to work basically two jobs, writing and my day job. I take care of the kids, keep the house clean, and cook every night for you since you don't eat leftovers, and try to keep my kids looking nice. You'd assume as a fellow mother and woman, she'd get that but no! The heffa..."

"Watch it." He stopped me.

"The...*woman*," I dragged the word out, "acts as if she doesn't understand. She just LOOKS for shit to call me on! All I'm trying to do is keep her son and grandchildren happy!"

"How did this even become a fight about us?"

"What?" I hissed.

"We were talking about hair, and you start getting into cleaning and cooking for me. And keeping me happy."

"I don't know, forget it. I'm not gonna be this hood couple fighting in the middle of an elementary school. I'm not gonna give them the satisfaction."

I pulled myself together. I'd dropped a bomb, acting as if I didn't see the mushroom cloud over the two of us. I wanted to say, "I'm killing myself so YOU can live while doing everything YOU want to do with YOUR life." But that statement had nothing to do with the argument at hand. Though his mother was a pain in my ass, she wasn't the most significant issue between Handsome McHandsomekins and me.

There were other issues, older issues that neither of us had addressed before we got married, rearing their ugly heads once again.

Out of nowhere, James insisted, "I'm going to the car real fast. I forgot something."

"Yeah, whatever. Alright. Fine." I grunted.

We parted ways, and I kept walking to the classroom. Maya was talking to my parents. My father held West's hand to keep him from running around the room. Maya and I locked eyes. She smiled and jumped.

"You were the sh..." I caught myself, remembering I was speaking to a child. "You were awesome, baby!"

"Where's Daddy?" Maya asked.

"He'll be right back, sweetheart. Don't worry."

HONNNNNKKK!

The light changed from red to green without me noticing. "Where are you rushing to go at two a.m.?" I demanded.

Boy, *this* trip couldn't have come at a better time. Usually, I'd be pissed about taking a 4 a.m. flight to Chicago, but after yesterday's

Chapter Three
My Daughter F***ing Rocks, Thank You Very
Much

fight, I wanted to spend as little time with James as possible. The gag is, I was speaking at a women's empowerment conference on work-life balance and marriage.

The irony that is my life...putting on a smile so other mothers can think work-life balance is indeed possible. Speaking of work-life balance, I planned to return home the same day to pick Maya and West up from Aunt Lisa. All this just to be able to tuck my babies into bed on the same night. Sigh... the sacrifices us working mamas make.

I love business trips for the alone time. I have the ability to go to restaurants where all the expenses are paid while not having a strict time schedule. I don't have to get anyone dressed, and I can go to the gym at my leisure. Yet, even if I did stay overnight, what would I have put on the TV in the hotel room?

Peppa Pig.

I'm pathetic.

I reached into my purse in the passenger seat, eyes still looking straight ahead to focus on the road. I rifled past the hand sanitizer, inhalers, wet wipes, and wallet to find Mecca...a mini package of Oreos.

I squealed! "YASSSS Bitcchhh!"

To this day, I can't think of a more fantastically gratifying stress reliever that the one manufactured by Nabisco. Over 100 years ago, their divine healers created this sandwich cookie consisting of two chocolate wafers perfected with a sweet creme filling in-between.

My greed caused me to fuck around and drop an Oreo while trying to remove it from the packaging. It fell from my lap to in-between the car seat and arm console. I hit the brakes, moving my hand around on the car floor while simultaneously watching the road and trying to find that cookie. When I saw it, I picked it up, kissed it, and lifted it up to God so he'd bless it with the five-second rule.

I smashed that little two inches of heaven, also known as my breakfast. I was utterly lost in the moment, caught up in the rapture until my cell phone started to ring. I let it sync with my car and answered it. Why am I getting a call this early in the morning?

"This is Christine," I stated.

"Hey."

DAMMIT! Well, if it wasn't *my* older issue rearing its ugly head. I needed to stop rushing to answer the phone before identifying the caller via the screen ID. I turned the audio on the call from the car speaker back to the iPhone.

"Hi. How are you?" I'm not too excited to have a conversation, but I have manners. "Why are you calling me at 2 a.m.? I am married, you know."

"But I knew you would answer. Or at least see the call. Are you avoiding my calls and texts?" he asked. I was, but I don't want to get into why on this call. He continues.

"You know what I just saw on TV? An ad for Champions of Courage. Remember when you won?"

"Yeah, I do," I mumbled. I honestly didn't feel like going down memory lane in the middle of the night.

"I knew you'd win," he said.

"What does *that* mean?" I hissed. If it's one thing I hate, it's being stereotyped. Even if it's not with negative intention, I still hate it. Especially from *him*.

"You're a perfectionist. If you set your mind to do something, it's going to be done—and done well," he added. "Plus, a chance to speak your mind on TV? Oh yeah, it was gonna get done," he laughed.

I hated it when he laughed at me, too. I was getting even more irritated and offended, so I decided to rush off the phone. "I gotta go. I'm headed to the airport and definitely can't do this right now," I say in one breath.

"I'll get off the phone. I was just thinking about the wonderful Christine Michel Epps." He calls me by my maiden name. I expected after all these years, he could bring himself to call me Carter. But perhaps it was because he couldn't bring himself to call me by another man's last name.

"Thank you," I smugly replied.

"Is James going with you?"

"No," I said.

"Oh, excuse me." He said with sass. "Well, why not?"

The last thing I want to do is share my marital problems, which only seemed to be escalating as the days went on, with this fool. I really didn't have a prepared answer to the question, so I lied. "He couldn't get off work. Aight. I gotta go. I'll call you later this evening."

"Alright. DON'T. FORGET. Put a reminder in your phone right now."

I hung up.

Truth be told, James could have come, but I didn't want him there. I knew where James would be while I was at the conference. The same place he always was; in the basement. He'd become a recluse and was having trouble sleeping through the night. Maya had even taken to calling him "grumpy Daddy," partly because of his frequent cynical, negative, and irritable responses in family discussions.

James could also pick up the kids and watch his own damn offspring for the evening. Sometimes I felt like I couldn't get this man to do anything that would help make my life a bit easier. Including being on my team.

When James solely focused on his career, I said nothing. Damn near bent over and folded into a stool so I could support his weight. Now that I'm focusing on my career, you'd think I'd get the same courtesy. But nope. I still gotta take care of him, the house and the kids. And I'm supposed to be happy?

Must be nice to do whatever the fuck you wanna do with no responsibilities, I ranted. I want him to wake up and actually give a shit about this marriage!

I turned up Travis Scott on the radio as I finally approached my exit. Lost in Astroworld, my emotions started to get the best of me. My body felt heavy. It seemed like lately, all I did was travel from one errand to the next, one project to the next...a rolling stone or wayfaring stranger traveling through this world below.

As I left the car in the parking lot, I reached into my purse again, but this time for my iPhone. I could use a great listener, and at this point, I didn't care who it was or where the empathy was coming from. I obviously couldn't have been killing it more as a professional. I mean, there I was headed to an event where they were going to be honoring ME for Christ's sake. The moment I set foot in an office—any office— I was a queen, comfortable and commanding in her castle.

So why was I allowing myself to become a chambermaid at home?

"Hey, Siri," I commanded, holding down the home button.

"Remind me to call WOMANIZER at 8 p.m. tonight."

When I found my seat on the plane, which should have been called a slingshot, it was so small—I noticed I was seated behind two newlyweds. How did I know? Oh, I don't know. Perhaps it was the matching bride and groom t-shirts that gave it away. Or maybe it was how they cozily sat side by side, resting on one another as they co-signed thank you notes to their bridal party.

"Jesus Christ. Is the whole fucking WORLD in love?" I scorned. Tell you what—it doesn't make me miss MY husband, though! But I do wish I was the kind of woman who wrote thank-you notes.

I could actually USE the opportunity to miss James. I was counting the minutes until the drink cart rolled around, and I could excuse ordering Jack Daniels and Coke for it being 5:00 somewhere. I mean, wasn't it still technically the evening? Shit. This is my only "me time."

I was physically and mentally far from my parental and domestic responsibilities. I was literally moving away from my husband. Admittedly these past few days had been a bit rough, but hopefully, this was just a bump in our road. Who knows? I might just have been in my feelings. I had been running around scatterbrained, tackling item by item from my to-do list. Maybe I just needed to add "being nice to Handsome McHandsomekins" back on it. Perhaps not. I didn't know.

I stared at the navy leather airplane seat in front of me and took a deep breath. It was 4 a.m. Today was a new day; so, today was a new me. I was so over being pulled in different directions. The only direction I wanted to move was FORWARD. I was up early and never felt more productive than I did in the mornings. A thought popped in my mind.

Make a list, Chrissy. Oooooo!

A list! Nothing turns my organized, Type A mind on more! Lists control my stress. And plus, they just look so damn Pinterest-worthy when written in cursive using black ink on colorful stationery.

Seriously, writing always calms my anxiety and puts things into perspective. Plus, this women's empowerment conference was inspiring me to focus on my strengths. I reached under one of the lovebird's airplane seats, pulling out my notebook and pen.

Look at me at 4 a.m., exploring ideas and shit.

I free wrote:

You are—and always have been—one boss ass bitch. Bitch, you graduated high school at 16, turning around the next day to start working a full-time government job.

Wait. I squinted my face at the paper. I didn't wanna curse at myself. *This is your Oprah moment, Christine. Think Oprah. Okay.*

You're street-smart and well-educated. You're paying back your college loans on your own (be them deferred LOL). You have achieved everything you have without a master's degree because you ain't got time to be doing your daughter's homework AND yours too.

That's better, I insisted.

You influence people's opinion of your hometown by being a smart, talented professional. People outside of Baltimore see your influence and respect your perspective. You bring credit and intelligence back to the city.

YASSSS!

You're a chameleon...

Oooo, not chameleon! C'mon, big words at 4 a.m.

...who has mastered the art of shutting up in meetings to seem cultured, intellectual, and pensive.

(Whole time shit is just going over your head, but still.)

You started a business. In the middle of a recession. And still thrived.

Bitch, WHAT?! Fuck Martin...you the Man of the Decade.

Chapter Three
My Daughter F***ing Rocks, Thank You Very
Much

Yeah, people either love or hate you, but no one is in a gray area. You don't network, or do small talk or polite convos. You're a straight shooter.

You actually VALUE business relationships. You remember the personal details people tell you not because you want to persuade or sell them, but because you genuinely care about the humans in the suits.

I took a look at the list and laughed. *Get it, girl,* I said to myself. Out here making it happen instead of sitting around and waiting for it to happen.

The plane started to take off as I reached for my purse in the seat next to me. I forgot to switch my phone to airplane mode. I touched the home button, and my screensaver appeared. An image of James, Maya, and West in downward dog on the kitchen floor.

I smiled.

I don't believe in coincidences.

I took my screen magically turning on as a sign. God doesn't like vanity, and he doesn't like ugly. I realized my gratitude list wasn't the type of list I needed to make. This list was entirely about everything I do (and have done) as a professional. But it doesn't mean jack shit.

There was nothing about James on this list. Yeah, I was stressed at home, and I couldn't remember what my husband's penis looked like. But was work legit becoming that much of an escape from reality? Was I only thankful for my career? Did I care only about the woman in my suit? Had I forgotten what was important?

I needed to reevaluate my priorities. I should have missed my husband right then, and I didn't. My career had too much power in my life. I wasn't giving myself enough freedom to grow and enjoy my family. This list needed to be amended.

Miss, my husband. Miss. Mission. Oh! What about a personal mission statement?

Ahhhh, I love it, Chrissy!

Okay, here we go.

The irony that is my life...putting on a smile so other mothers can think work-life balance is indeed possible.

CHAPTER FOUR

GUESS WE'RE NOT F***ING

Mommy, can you open this for me?" Maya yelled over the shower door, interrupting both my shower and my train of thought. Through the steam, I could see her holding an apple juice box and a plastic pink cell phone.

"You're supposed to be taking your nap! And I'm in the shower! Ask Daddy."

"I did. He told me to ask you."

Of course. Everybody in this house can hear the got damn shower running, yet somehow, I'm supposed to still answer their beck and call.

"Would you come on? I'm on a conference call!"

"Girl!" I snapped. "You're five years old. What do you know about a conference call? You better NOT talk to me that way! I don't care *what* you're on!"

I cracked open the shower door, and Maya handed me the juice box. I ripped the straw out of the plastic and inserted it. "Here."

Maya grabbed the juice and walked out of the bathroom. "I'm back," she sighed into the phone.

This child. "Are you gonna take this plastic trash and shut the bathroom door?"

Why did I even bother asking that question? I was already being ignored.

Just moments before I stepped back into the shower, I stepped on Rubble AGAIN with my bare foot. As usual, I yelled, "FUUUCCCKKKK!!!!" But that time, I gave up. I looked at the ceiling with defeat. I'd been toying with the idea of creating a personal mission statement for a few days ever since I got back from Chicago, and actually, I thought it may have legs. It may have been uptight and anal to create a personal mission statement, or perhaps it was practical and methodical. Either way, I decided to take it one step further and put my Type A personality to good use. Before Maya interrupted my train of thought, I'd settled on the fact that work was straight. I needed to focus on these kids and my husband.

I got out the shower and dried off, looking in the mirror at the US road system, also known as the stretch marks on my stomach from two pregnancies.

Better add my health to the mission statement, I grunted.

I wrapped my towel around my armpits and plopped on my bed. Reaching into the drawer on my side of the bed, I pulled out a pen and used envelope. I jotted a few words that came to mind on the back:

Healthy. Fit. Connect. Guidance. Discipline. Sex. Balance. Fitness. Love. Joy. Happiness. Winning. Passion. Life.

I toyed around with word combinations, phrases, and sentences. Ultimately, one hour later, I came up with three sentences that addressed the parts of my life where I was a mess.

• Be a loving, present mother who balances fun with fundamentals to guide disciplined, gracious, educated, spiritual children.

• Be healthy, fit, and reaping the benefits of doing so; not accepting hereditary and periodic ailments or physical obstacles.

• Consistently connecting with my husband, being thrilled by his presence, and experiencing sensual passion.

Yeesh, I gulped. This shit is a **BHAG** (big, hairy, aggressive goal) like a motherfucker!

I decided to start with the two hardest—go big or go home, right? I assumed if my kids saw a fit mother who was in love with their father, they'd turn out aight in the end. I mean, I once read a mother's physical activity can set a powerful example for young girls. Plus, I could hear Maya and West arguing over who could watch their TV show next in the family room. I surely wasn't in the mood to do anything to enrich their lives at that moment.

So, it was be healthy, fit, and reaping the benefits of doing so; not accepting hereditary and periodic ailments or physical obstacles and consistently connecting with my husband, being thrilled by his presence and experiencing sensual passion.

Sure, I already had a gym membership and went pretty frequently. Well, shit, enough. But working out wasn't my obstacle. It was stress eating. And in addition to stress eating, I have a plethora of mental roadblocks. I'm afraid that damn black man's disease—diabetes—is going to creep up on me. Will I ever fully overcome my childhood relationship with junk food? It's hard to forget decades of poor eating! How am I supposed to be the healthiest and most fit version of myself, with so little guidance growing up and a family with a shitty medical record? I wish it were true, but it took me nearly a decade to learn oxygen alone does not exert your body. I've already dealt with a high cholesterol diagnosis in college. What's around the corner next? Not sleeping regularly and drinking a glass and a half to two glasses of wine each night is not helping me live a healthy lifestyle either, let me tell you.

Buttt...I once read women with healthier lifestyles have more sex. So, maybe starting with this would help my other goal to "experience sensual pleasure" with James.

Eating eggplant will get me more eggplant...I pondered. What better reason is there to eat healthy? Win-win!

I'll go to the gym tomorrow but tonight...we feast on eggplant.

That evening, it seemed as if it took forever to put the kids to bed. It was still the usual tug of war. ("I want my last sip! You didn't read the whole story! I want one more hug!"), but I was excited to work on the husband task in my mission statement. I'd snuck a tube of Vaseline baby gel in my bedroom drawer, and I had a plan.

Children are expert cockblockers. They will create extraordinary incidents to prevent their parents from having romantic, passionate moments. They make having sex tricky. Very tricky. Aside from chasing them around the house (draining my energy), they don't exactly encourage coitus with their loud-volume TV shows and annoying questions.

But we were NOT gonna be the stereotypical couple, sitting across from each other in Panera Bread in matching monochromatic Lands' End sweaters silently reading the Washington Post. You KNOW they're not going home and having sex in any different position but missionary. I didn't want that for us too. We were in our thirties. We still had hot years ahead of us.

I'd spent Saturday afternoon changing the aura of my bedroom: I'd added some candles I'd found in a spare drawer, threw out all my mom panties (the ones that could also serve as a second diaper bag they're so big), and removed all photos of my kids. I felt I'd genuinely returned the bedroom to its natural glory of being an adult oasis. I decided then-and-there that if a child came into my bedroom with a toy, they weren't allowed to let it linger on the dresser or on a nightstand. Otherwise, it was tossed. I did NOT want to turn my head to the side and see Doc McStuffins creepily smiling at me while I was getting head.

After Maya and West felt they'd gotten enough bullshit out of me before bedtime, I tiptoed down the hallway, down the stairs and into the basement to find James watching ESPN.

"James," I attempted to say in a sultry tone from the steps, "can you come upstairs?"

"I'm good down here," he dismissed. He had a Miller Lite in one hand, a remote in the other, and was barely paying attention to the TV.

"Why don't you want to come upstairs?"

"I'm unwinding down here," he replied.

From what? I thought. He'd been in the basement all Saturday afternoon and evening, a recluse in his chilly, dark man cave. I'd been listening to who hit who and who was hungry for what all day long! Still, I was on a mission and sick of being coy. I cut to the chase.

"Come upstairs so we can fuck goddammit."

He groaned, slamming his beer on the table beside him. Putting the remote down, he rose from the sofa. I turned and stomped up the steps. Standing by the bed in the bedroom, I waited until I heard him shuffle up the last stairs. I grinned.

"Look at what I got." I sang.

"Oh, Jesus," he laughed. "What are you going to do with that?"

"We're going to try anal!" I belted excitedly! "Oh yeah."

(I had a long way to go before my sex talk was up there with the likes of the women on Pornhub, so shoot me.) We'd never done it before, and I believed switching things up would make all the difference.

James slipped off his briefs. I took off my robe, jumped on the bed, and kneeled in one motion, my forearms and knees spread like a frog about to leap. I heard the cap pop off the gel, and we were off to the races.

Or so I thought.

"JESUS CHRIST. IS THAT THE RIGHT HOLE?" I screamed. He was trying to force an Almond Joy into a pencil sharpener.

"Shhhh!" James laughed. "You're gonna wake the kids! And you only have two holes I'm going for the one I never go in!"

"OWWWWW! I CAN'T DO THIS! FUCK THIS! HOW DO WOMEN DO THIS? MAYBE WE NEED MORE GEL!"

"Aight!"

He tried to enter again, and the pressure nearly cracked my booty hole.

"Naw, man; fuck this," I yelled, shaking my head like a toddler.

No, don't give up.

"HoldonjustHOLDON!" I shouted in one breath.

And on and on that dance went for about 15 minutes, until we ran out of gel and interest.

I rolled on my back, while James stood over the side of the bed, smirking and shaking his head.

"Well, at least I tried!" I felt embarrassed. "What are YOU doing? You know we're not in a good place."

James looked at me with confusion. "How is this supposed to help us get back to a good place, Christine?" he asked.

I looked to the side and shrugged, "I don't know. I thought trying something new would be sensual and passionate and all that. I'm trying!" I replied.

James put his briefs back on and turned his back to me. "I'm going back downstairs."

I laid there on my back, spread eagle, lubed up like rotisserie chicken...and sighed. We were in a bind. He wanted sex to feel connected, but I wanted to feel connected to have sex. And round and round we went.

I climbed under the covers, too lazy to put on my pajamas, and reached for my phone. I texted Womanizer.

"What's been going on with you these past couple weeks?"

Three dots pulsed.

"Just been working, raising kids. U?"

Womanizer was a single dad and had never married. I'd always admired his tendency to go against what society thought was best for people and to carve his own path. He'd taken custody of his children and worked hard as an entrepreneur to provide for them.

I'd often wondered how hard it was for him to handle single parenting on his own, feeling sad that even though he was a cheater and a liar and always on fuck boy shit (from a romantic perspective), he never found a wife. It's not like he wasn't attractive. His walnut skin was a lovely finishing touch to his muscular frame, I assure you. Jesus. Here I am sounding like a got damn romance novel writer, but the man is fine. Shit.

"Trying to work on my marriage," I deeply exhaled as I typed the sentence, proceeding to explain the night's event.

"LOLOLOLOLOL," he replied. "Marriage is tough, I hear. At least you gave it a shot...in the ass! LOLOLOLOL."

"Haha, hell," I wrote back.

The next morning, I woke up with an instant headache. Sunday morning had arrived, and my in-laws were coming by to plan their family reunion with James. Rolling to the side, I looked at the bedroom wall.

Fucking kill me now, I thought.

With one hand on the mattress, I lifted myself up and groaned as I sat up and stared at the same wall. I looked over my shoulder, discovering James wasn't in bed with me. He'd no doubt passed out in the basement. I walked down the stairs and halfway into the basement. Sure enough, there he was on the sofa, next to four beer cans and leftovers I'd cooked Saturday night.

Walking all the way down the stairs and grabbing the trash, I kicked the side of his chin to wake him up. He didn't move.

"James. James. James!" I yelled.

He slowly opened his eyes. "Huh? What?"

"Your parents are on their way. You gotta watch the kids so I can go to the gym. Get up."

I walked back up the stairs, throwing the trash away. Both kids had broken free from their cocoon of pillows and were in their rooms watching cartoons. If I moved fast, I could get my gym clothes on without them noticing. Last night's sex romp didn't exactly work, so I was on to the next part of my mission statement of being healthy, fit, and reaping the benefits of doing so; not accepting hereditary and periodic ailments or physical obstacles.

I also wanted to get out of the house before I ran into Mother-in-law- ificent. She didn't need to see the tension between James and me, because she'd feel the need to jump in and give her old-school bullshit two cents.

I threw on a sports bra, tank top, and yoga pants. I slipped into some flip flops and flew down the stairs. With this headache, yoga was just what I needed to bring me back to chill.

"James," I whispered into the basement with the fear that a child would come to find me and ask what I was doing. "I'm leaving to go to the gym!"

I grabbed my keys and purse and walked out of the back kitchen door.

"Shit!" I'd grabbed James keys instead of mine. *It's okay. I'll take his car.*

Getting inside his SUV, I immediately balked at the amount of trash in it. Fast food wrappers, wrinkled dress shirts in the passenger seat, old soda can syrup and old...*boxes filled with beer cans?* "What the fuck is all this?" I hissed.

Argh...I'm not dealing with this now. I'm going to the gym.

According to contributor Dr. David Ryan, to achieve general fitness, there is no need to separate body parts on any given day. You can train your entire body, three to four times a week, performing two to three exercises per body part, with 12 to 15 repetitions per set. This will produce a trained fitness individual and give you the basic level of fitness that you would need to maintain or establish, before obtaining higher fitness goals.

When the fuck am I supposed to do that? I huffed, thumbing through Muscle & Fitness Magazine in the yoga studio lobby.

"Leslie!" a woman called out to another lady sitting next to me. We both looked up.

"Hi, Molly. How are you? How are the kids?"

How are you? How are the kids? I whined in my head. *Baltimore. More like carbon copy Smalltimore.* It seemed as though every woman in Baltimore decided to do the same yoga class at the same time because they all knew each other. No matter their age or the time of day I was there.

I often wondered: Does one of them blow a conch shell-like Ron Burgundy in *Anchorman 2* outside of a Lululemon or something to signal the others? I didn't get it! They were always ecstatic to be at the gym and in each other's company every time I went! I'd be panting like crazy, rolling my eyes and spitting sweat as I greeted them in the locker room, but they were cheerfully conversing amongst each other, giggling about what their plans after they left the gym.

"Welcome to Body Flow, everyone. I'm Regina, your instructor. Is this anyone's first time or first time back after a while?"

Everybody looked at me as if we were in church, and they asked who the guest worshippers were. They knew I was a new face, but I'd be damned if I was gonna embarrass myself. I kept my eyes straight ahead, looked at the teacher, and smiled.

"Let me just adjust the music, and we'll begin," Regina whispered.

A soft, ethereal cover of Pink's *What About Us* started to play through the speakers. Taking a deep breath, I exhaled.

Let's get this "me time" started. I'd forgotten how marvelous this moment felt—the absence of a husband or children. The gym is cathartic for me. After I leave, I always get that feeling you feel in your chest after crying.

I can't see them coming down my eyes, so I gotta make my yoga pants cry.

We started the warm-up sequence, and I noticed the tension in my body. It's difficult for me to adjust to the way my body is changing as

I'm aging, and it's not just about fitting into pre-baby clothes. From my soft belly to my depressed tits to my back fat, I'm not ecstatic with the way I look. I thought with the mission statement (and if the disaster that was last night taught me anything) I was gonna start off small. I would commit to the gym one day a week, going for thirty minutes each week. Then, I would add a day and one more day until I reached five days a week. I didn't wanna work out to look a certain way, but I did want to control my eating and exercise routine.

In warrior two pose, I looked at the woman to the right of me. She was size two with NO BACK FAT, not a roll protruding from any part of her thin-strapped tank top.

Wish I could wear thin straps, I thought. Quickly my inner critic reminded me. *Bitch, how?*

I looked around the room at all the women. Maybe I just wasn't meant to be there. I felt like they all were comfortable being in the gym, and my anxiety was on full display. None of them had 1/3 of their body fat sitting on top of their ribs like I did. They didn't look like after this workout, their thigh muscles were gonna be so sore it'd be virtually impossible to sit...and thus shit...on a toilet.

I transitioned into big toe, coming face-to-ass with the black woman to the left of me. *Good God, woman!* Confession: Sometimes, I ogled other black women at the gym. Blame it on the pigment. I'd suck my teeth and grin:

Damn girl! Why are you here? You too fine to be sweating up in this gym with me! Look at your boobs sitting up and shit. What child forgot to deliberately drain the life force out of your titties? Why are you trying to lose all that ass that I would sell my soul to the devil to have? You can do side bends or sit-ups. But please don't lose that butt.

Focus, Christine; focus.

"Root down through the feet. Open the heart and find the breath." Regina whispered in my ear.

Chapter Four
Guess We're Not F***ing

I jumped. Damn, this bitch is STEALTH! What am I gonna cook tonight for dinner? My mind wandered.

The class was over in no time, and I was no less stressed. In fact, all I did most of Body Flow was wince in pain and complain internally about how fat I was. What a waste.

Grabbing my phone from my purse in the locker, I saw I had ten missed calls and two missed texts from James. My heart raced. I could feel the blood moving through my legs, grounding me in that spot. The kids!

I called him back, and Maya answered.

"Hi, Mommy!" she gushed.

"Hi, baby," the sound in her voice calmed me for a second. "Where's Daddy, honey? He called me a bunch of times."

"No, he didn't call you. That was Maw Maw. Daddy had to ride in the ambulance."

"WHAT?!"

We were in a bind. He wanted sex to feel connected, but I wanted to feel connected to have sex. And round and round we went.

Chapter Four
Guess We're Not F***ing

CHAPTER FIVE

YOUR F***ING BLACK CRACKS...ON THE INSIDE

G ood afternoon. I'm here to see a patient who was just brought in by the ambulance. I'm his wife. He might still be in the emergency room. His name is James Carter. Thank you so much."

My words came out breathy from running inside the hospital and fighting the cold January air, but I still got polite as fuck when I was freaked out.

The woman searched the hospital database and smiled. "Yes, he's still in the emergency room. Let me call back there and see if I can take you back."

Just then, out the corner of my eye, I saw a little girl with purple and brown braids singing.

"Nothing can stop me. I'm all the way up!" she sang.

"MAYA!" I yelled, the people in the waiting area staring at me. "Come here, baby."

"Mommy!" she yelled, running to me. Clearly, at that point, neither of us cared that we were in a hospital. My eyes focused a bit more, and I could see she was sitting with James' father and West.

The woman got off the phone. "He's back there but already has a visitor who is refusing to leave his side."

Hagatha, I hissed to myself. "Well, as his wife and the person responsible for this hospital bill when he leaves, I'll be going back to speak with his doctor and see James privately. Thank you."

The woman smiled, though she was clearly confused. She gave me a badge and directions to get to James' room. I thanked her and walked down the hall.

As if my mind wasn't racing already, now I had to deal with *this* bitch. We hated each other more than Tupac and Biggie; more than Jay-Z and Nas. There was NO squashing our beef. I was tolerable until the day James decided to marry me. Then, she'd gone so far on my wedding day to tell my grandmother I was a bitch before leaving the wedding early. Over the years, she had done everything from ignoring my requests to give her grandchildren their asthma medication during sleepovers to gossiping about me—on my got damn couch—after my annual Christmas brunch.

Yes, we couldn't tolerate one another. And now she'd beaten me to the hospital, which made her believe she was in control of the situation. But no one takes control from me.

A doctor started to cross my path, walking into the hospital room I was jogging towards. "Excuse me," I asked, "are you James Carter's doctor?"

"I am," he replied. "I was just about to go visit him. Are you his wife?"

"Yes. What happened?"

"I can't share that information with you per the request of his family, but he's coming to. Perhaps he'll say different."

The doctor seemed uncomfortable uttering such a dumbass reply, but I got it. The devil had stressed him and the staff out so much and demanded so much, he'd given in just to shut her up. After all these years, I'd become comfortable with dealing with innocent bystanders like this doctor.

"Fine," I smiled. I followed the doctor into the room and pulled back the privacy curtain.

I gasped. Where was Handsome McHandsomekins?

My once mahogany-colored husband was devoid of color. Sadness clouded his features; the warmth of his skin had been replaced with ash. It was hard for a dark-skinned man to be pale, but somehow, James had successfully done it. I noticed he was thinner than usual the night before, but looking at him in the hospital bed, I saw how frail and weak his body had become.

"Hey, babe." James slowly turned his head, barely able to open his eyes. "I'm sorry to pull you away from work."

"I...wasn't...at work." Suddenly I became acutely aware of how warm the room was. My fingers were ice-cold, yet I could feel the sweat on the back of my neck. This was my baby I was looking at, lying defenseless in a hospital bed.

The sound of someone clearing their throat brought me back from being detached. Hagatha.

"Can I speak with James privately?" *Bitch*, I wanted to add at the end of that sentence.

She just stared at me, readjusting her ugly fat ass in the hospital chair.

"Ma, can I speak to Christine, please?" The fact that James had to ask while speaking in his low and hoarse voice pissed me off even further.

"Fine, but I'm coming back in an hour," she huffed, brushing past me as she left the room.

Chapter Five
Your F***ing Black Cracks...On the Inside

Are you fucking kidding me?

"Baby, what happened?" I asked, James still unable to make eye contact.

"Your husband had a seizure," the doctor replied. I'd forgotten he was in the room.

"What?"

The doctor continued. "Mr. Carter, do you remember anything before the seizure? Anything from the moment you woke up?"

"No."

What? We'd had a whole conversation that morning!

"Were you drinking?" The doctor continued.

"Not that much," James replied slowly.

"How much is not that much?" The doctor asked.

"I think I had two beers or so," James whispered, knowing that was a lot for a Sunday morning. And a lie. Plus, I knew it was a continuation from last night because he was irritable about me interrupting his drinking the night before.

"Mr. Carter, your blood work does show you were drinking quite heavily. The fact that you can't remember the morning concerns me a bit, as well. Do you have a problem with alcohol?"

"No, I only drink when I'm stressed," James answered.

Yes, I answered matter-of-factly in my head. I started to put two-and-two together, and an overwhelming fear emerged. James always had a beer in his hand; hell, even as he passed a liquor store advertising his favorite brand of alcohol, Maya would yell, "That's what Daddy drinks!" But what I'd just realized was that he was drinking alone, in that cold basement, on his sofa bed. And way too much.

Before we were married, he had problems with his consumption, attributing it to stress from studying for his certified public accountant (CPA) exam. Thinking about that time and the horror of his unpredictable moods gave me a nauseating feeling all over again. But then the doctor interrupted my train of thought.

"Mr. Carter," he continued, obviously ignoring James' response to the question. "Being stressed is normal. But stress that occurs too often or for too long can cause problems, thereby interfering with normal daily activities. It can weaken your immune system and increase your risk of physical illness. Curing stress with alcohol—especially as a husband and father—is dangerous. That's an unhealthy behavior that comes with its own host of stuff, including anger, starvation, insomnia, low energy, and depression."

Just then, my Aunt Lisa appeared in the doorway. I'd forgotten I'd called her from the car to tell her what was happening and where I was going. James was her adopted baby. There was no way I was going to be able to keep her from seeing him.

"Hi, baby. I love you." Aunt Lisa walked over to James and gave him a kiss.

"Hi, Aunt Lisa. I love you too."

She rubbed my back, letting me know I'd be okay. It was as if her hand was a warmed, healing stone. It instantly made me breathe deeply and become cognizant of my emotions. I exhaled and started to calm myself down.

"Mrs. Carter, do you mind if I continue the conversation for just a few minutes with only Mr. Carter?" the doctor asked.

"Of course." I exited the room with Aunt Lisa, and we stood outside in the hall.

"What's going on? How are you?" she asked.

Just then, I felt my phone vibrating in my purse. I peeked inside of it and could see the screen. WOMANIZER. I tucked the purse under my arm, letting it vibrate.

"I'm fine," I quickly answered, attempting to sound upbeat. Aunt Lisa carried the weight of so many other people's issues. She was the glue that held everyone's lives together: her kids, her husband, MY kids, and MY husband. I didn't want to add my stress onto her plate.

"I'm going to ask again," she asked in a way only black mothers could. "How are you?"

I'm trying to keep myself together. My heart is palpitating, and I'm choking at the same time. Yet, I'm standing here talking to you like it's nothing. I want to move full steam ahead from this and move past it. Continue rocking and rolling in my world. But I can't help to think my husband is gonna kill me. Like he wants to see me fail. He's betrayed me. I know it's not true, but we have such perfect babies and a perfect connection. Still, he's blocking me from living a perfect life. I've never felt so alone in my life, and yet, so aware of how bad three other people in my house need me. My knees are weak.

"I'm fine," I replied instead. "Just trying to see what's going on with James." I couldn't say all that to her.

She leaned against the wall. "Do you want to talk about it? Because if I were you and your uncle was laying in that bed, with that monster I passed in the waiting room breathing down my neck, I'd be a wreck. I'll stay right here, okay?" Aunt Lisa was clearly hoping I'd realize I was in the midst of a crisis.

I chuckled, "Yeah, I know, right? I'm good. Stuff is crazy." I dismissed her concern. "But I gotta just hear what the doctor says and keep moving, right?"

Adults really become adults at pivotal moments. James isn't just handy when the kids get beads stuck up their nose. He's been there for each of my pivotal moments (from college to entrepreneurship to the death of my grandparents). I literally didn't know how to adult without him. I was beyond concerned. My life lay in that hospital bed eight feet away from me.

"Here we go."

At the persistent (and I do mean persistent) request of my aunt, I stood two days later at the front door of a therapist. She'd sent me seven text messages and called three times that Sunday after we left James in the hospital, demanding I go. I'd researched a therapist who could deal with family issues because I was under the impression that my family *was* my issue. And so, I came across Jennifer Sober. Jesus must've genuinely wanted me to go because she had an open appointment for that Tuesday morning.

You know how people say, "I had no idea what to expect." I knew what to expect. She was gonna give me some rah-rah bullshit and send me on my way. Or, she was gonna recommend I discuss a prescription for Lorazepam with my physician. I didn't need either. I figured I'd go just to tell my aunt I went, go across the street to CVS, grab some ashwagandha and a Snickers bar, and be fine. Shit.

I just needed to get better control over my life and execute this damn mission statement. The proof would be in the pudding, and things would turn around. I really believed that. Things would turn around.

I opened the door. "Hi! Christine?"

Jennifer was so lovely, warm, and welcoming. But white. Oh dear.

"Hi! Jennifer?"

Now, I'm a realist. I understand the chances of me finding a black female millennial therapist in Cockeysville, Maryland, is virtually impossible. I don't have a problem with receiving the advice of, confiding in, or shooting the shit with white women. But this was supposed to be therapy, and I'm supposed to let it all out.

How could I candidly discuss all my "issues"—why I have such a Type A personality; why my husband feels so stressed in corporate

Chapter Five
Your F***ing Black Cracks...On the Inside

America; why I put so much pressure on myself; why I'm always concerned about the safety and education of my children, etc.—to someone who has no idea what it's like to live in my world?

I responded. "How are you? Should I come right into your office?"

"Sure, come on in!" Jennifer was so kind. I had to find a way to stop being prejudiced (because that's exactly what I was being). I hated it when people were that way to me. So, I let this woman do her job. "So, what brings you to see me in such a rush?"

"My aunt was the rush!" I chuckled. "I know I have things to work on, and I think I can handle them by myself. But she thinks I need to talk about them."

"Does she know what you need to work on?" Jennifer asked.

"No," I answered.

"But she thinks you just have things you should talk about."

"Right." Okay; Jennifer, I know I can be confusing, so bonus points to you for speaking Christine!

"Can you tell me about what you need to work on?" Jennifer got comfy in her chair, awaiting my reply.

"Well, I have a hectic life. I'm a writer and marketing strategist and mother, and wife. I've got a lot going on." Jennifer grinned happily, waiting for me to continue.

"I work an erratic and demanding schedule since I technically have two full-time jobs. Obviously, this makes being a mother all the more challenging. Sometimes, my patience with them wears thin. My patience with my husband runs even thinner, and we virtually have no conversation outside of our kids. We used to be best friends, but recently we've grown apart. We have the worst sex when we do have it; and, just recently, he had a seizure from drinking too much. Oh, and before all this happened, I decided to make a life to-do list since I am a writer—a mission statement. It's to improve my attitude and life. I want to spend more time with my kids while being fit and healthy. I also eat like shit, by the way. Can I curse?"

Jennifer nodded.

"...and reconnect with my husband. But I'm confident that if I just do all that, my life will be great."

"Wow," she exclaimed. "That's a lot to say in one breath! But you have clearly stated it well...wow." Jennifer wrote feverishly on her iPad. "Where do we start?"

I laughed. "Yeah, I guess I'm a mess. Still, it's my mess, and I know it well."

"Have you ever sought help in dealing with 'your mess'?" Jennifer put the last two words in air quotes.

"I'm a pretty open book and constantly looking for ways to improve myself. So, I'm always listening to Ted talks, reading articles about motherhood and professional development, and looking at data for the articles I write. So yeah, I am." I stated.

"But how is all that being an open book? I can see how it's seeking help, but that information is being said 'to you.' It's not a dialogue," Jennifer clarified.

"Oh, yeah. Naw, I don't discuss my shit," I replied, forgetting I was in mixed company. See, this is why I felt like I was gonna have problems coming to a therapist.

Jennifer appeared to be caught off guard by my causal response, but she asked: "Why not?"

I struggled to find a phrase or colloquialism that would explain my reasoning, but then she interrupted my train of thought. "Just don't feel comfortable letting the curtain fall?"

In a sense, Jennifer was right. It wasn't as if skin tone actually mattered. I wasn't letting the black people in my life in, much less the white ones. It didn't matter what color Jennifer was when I walked in the door; I just didn't let people in. I felt as though I could solve my own problems.

Damn. Ten minutes into this therapy session, and I'm I've already hit with an A-ha! moment, I smirked.

"Your current solutions may not be helping you emotionally. They're very logical and tactical, which I can clearly see is how you like to operate. You're a very successful woman. But you may have to step away from the logic and get to the emotional. The real. Logic has a way of helping us move past emotions, full steam ahead."

This bitch is in my head! Get out!

I love her. She's my new best friend.

"Alright," I responded with a nod, determined to play it cool.

"Have you ever been diagnosed with anxiety?" Jennifer started writing again on her iPad.

"Yes, I was. Shortly after, I gave birth to my daughter." I answered, clearing my throat as though something was lodged in it.

That was a sensitive subject for me, my weakness.

I had a horrible pregnancy and delivery with Maya. I discovered at week 30 that I'd had preëclampsia, and by week 30, day four, I was having contractions. I had no idea. I thought my legs were just locking up when I walked. I was admitted into the hospital, and for four days, I suffered through magnesium breathing treatments and shots in my ass. I finally gave birth to a two-pound, fifteen-ounce baby at thirty-one weeks and one day.

Something in me changed after I heard my daughter was in the NICU, laying in a glass case receiving food from a tiny tube. That she could barely keep on a preemie diaper. When I was asked if I wanted to see her, I said no. I wasn't in a rush, and other friends and family members could. I didn't realize I'd become detached from the world, just as I was when I saw James in the hospital present day. I didn't even know I was exhibiting a form of fear; the fear of becoming attached to Maya and having her die on me. I'd become a new woman, a mother, and full of anxiety.

"Most of the time, I can control it; so, I never feel like it stops me." I dismissed my thoughts.

"You know the interesting thing about anxiety," Jennifer added, "is that sometimes we think we can stop it, but it's like stopping the flood with a finger to the wall. So much in your life has changed since you gave birth, I imagine."

I nodded in shame, looking down at the bubbles in my cup of coffee.

Jennifer continued. "Perhaps your anxiety has moved from bad to worse. I don't think achieving everything on your mission statement will solve your issues, but I know your life can't continue this way. You need real change."

"Yeah, I know," I responded.

"Especially as a black woman," Jennifer added.

Bitch what? I got defensive and furrowed my eyebrows.

Jennifer clarified. "Black don't crack...on the outside."

Ok, Jennifer, I see you! Been outside of Cockeysville! I let her continue. "Black women age faster than white women on the inside. As successful as you are, you're more likely to experience stressful situations like workplace and public discrimination, and multiple caregiving roles. We've discussed just a few of those instances in the 40 minutes we've been in here. All that stress causes wear and tear on your internal organs, contributing to heart disease, high blood pressure, and stroke—all diseases of aging. Your black cracks on the inside."

Chapter Five
Your F***ing Black Cracks...On the Inside

She threw me off with that one, but I loved this woman. I looked outside the window at the morning dew on the green grass and saw a beautifully-coated deer.

Are you kidding me, God? I thought. I chuckled. This was a sign.

"What?" Jennifer asked.

"Nothing," I replied. "No, you know what? In the spirit of being transparent and actually trying to work on myself, I'll answer. I just saw a deer, and it's kind of a coincidence a deer appeared as we'd be discussing this. I sometimes have dreams where something in the future happens, something mundane and dumb. Nothing that tells the future too much. Anyway, I had a dream like that a couple days ago, the first night my husband was in the hospital. But it wasn't me."

"Continue," Jennifer looked puzzled.

"It was me, but it wasn't me. I dreamt of a deer trying to run through a house, to avoid a hunter. She was rushing to find her two baby deer, hoisting them up into a tree to safety before the hunter came. I woke up sweating and scared. I immediately thought of my children and me as the deer."

"Huh. And since you love research, I'll share this with you," Jennifer grinned. "It's been said dreaming of someone breaking into your house can suggest that you are feeling violated. It could also refer to a particular relationship or current situation in your life. Some subconscious material is attempting to make itself known. Some aspects of yourself that you have denied."

I exhaled loudly and nodded, sipping my coffee afterward. "I can see that."

I'm going to have to shoot this demon sorceress because she's in my head. I can't believe I've been here now 50 minutes. The time just flew by!

"Let's end here today. I'd love to see you again, and not just for the copay," Jennifer winked.

I smiled. "Yeah, we vibed, and I didn't think we would. Let's make another appointment."

I still wasn't 100% convinced seeing a therapist would solve my problems, but the discussion was interesting. In between appointments, it wouldn't hurt to take matters into my own hands and keep working on the mission statement.

Later that evening, with James still in the hospital, I decided to have some mommy and me time with Maya and West. I surprised the kids by picking them up from Aunt Lisa instead of having her drop them off. Maya jogged out the door to my Ford Explorer and hopped in the back seat, her brother wobbling behind her.

"Maya, you know I need to get out of the car before you come racing out the door. Your brother is following you. What's to stop him from going into the street?" I scolded.

"Sorry, Mommy," she replied.

"How was school?" I asked, still exhausted and reeling from therapy and a day of work.

"Good. Mommy look what I made in—"

"I think I'm going to take us to the Red Robin in White Marsh instead of Towson," I interrupted, picking up West and putting him into his car seat. I didn't wait for her answer. I locked him in, shut his door, and headed into the driver's seat. My eyes were fixed straight ahead on the road.

A half-hour in traffic and we arrived at Red Robin. I couldn't wait another minute to be at the restaurant, because if I had to hear "I'm hungry! Are we there yet?" one more time, I was going to shoot myself. Why do these kids feel we can make food magically appear?

Chapter Five
Your F***ing Black Cracks...On the Inside

You know how long I had to wait for food when I was little? It appears when it appears, dammit!

What a fantastic concept Red Robin is. Bottomless fries. Wowza. The kid in me loved Red Robin as much as Maya and West did. Because I didn't grow up eating "food," the nourishing substance that is consumed to sustain life, provide energy, and promote growth, I grew up on "FOOOOODDD." When I say this, it should conjure thoughts of all things fried, cured, smoked, and marinated. I'm talking savory, salt-heavy, and carb-loaded comfort foods. Red Robin has plenty of them.

But this was going to be an exciting trip to Red Robin because I was back to working on one of the mission statement tasks: be healthy, fit, and reaping the benefits of doing so; not accepting hereditary and periodic ailments or physical obstacles. And ain't no way in hell an onion ring tower (which I DEFINITELY was going to get and eat solo) was healthy.

We sat right down after entering, and since we came as a family oh, I don't know, about five times a month, we knew exactly what we wanted to order.

"Hi, my name is Paul. I'll be serving you guys today. Any allergies I should be aware of?"

"Yes, West is lactose-intolerant and has an egg allergy," I stated. "But we also already know what we'd like to order: she'll have the Cluck-A-Doodles and a Sprite. He'll just have some of the bottomless fries. I will, as well, with Thai chili sauce on the side. Please bring those out with my appetizer, an Onion Ring Tower."

Paul continued writing fervently.

"For my main meal...hold on." I remembered the mission statement. It feels virtually impossible to accommodate everyone's food preferences while keeping health and wellness top of mind, including my own. I grabbed my phone from my purse, unlocked it, and opened the MyFitnessPal app. I dictated:

"Tap 'Add to Diary.' Choose your meal: Dinner. Search for Onion Ring Tower."

At this point, I could see Paul looking at his other tables, worried he was taking up too much time with me. Plus, the kids were growing impatient and starving like Marvin.

Fuck it. "Paul, I'll take the Onion Ring Tower and the Royal Red Robin Burger."

"Alright, but just so you know—" I interrupted Paul. "I know, I know. Thanks!"

I had no idea what Paul was going to say and figured it wouldn't stop the kids from eating. That, after all, was currently the number one task at hand. We put away our menus, and I started to talk to Maya while West was occupied with a Ryder and Chase figurine.

I truly love my children. I pour everything into these cute faces and work so hard because they're innocent creatures. They've done nothing to hurt me. Maya likes to dress like *Clarissa Explains it All* and West looks cutest when he's dressed like an NBA basketball player at the strip club. And you know what? I'm here for both. I love them. Damn kids got me emotional.

Maya had carried something into the restaurant, and I hadn't even noticed. "Mommy, can I show you what I made now in school?"

"Of course, baby!" I beamed excitedly.

She handed me the folded purple construction paper. It was a card saying that she loves when I spend time with her because I'm fun, funny, silly, and loving. I loved it. It was the greatest gift ever, but... I decided I gotta give out more beatings. I'm not feared enough. I chuckled.

"Thanks, baby; it's awesome! Give me a hug I love you so much!"

We continued talking about the shit that little kids love to talk about, making a 15-minute wait for food feel like an hour.

Chapter Five
Your F***ing Black Cracks...On the Inside

"Mommy, I told people my mother's name is Christine in school today." Maya joked.

"Eww, Maya. Don't say that," I teased. "It makes me sound like a grown-up."

"You ARE a grown-up, silly!" I winked at her, and we laughed.

Our food arrived, and the kids dug in. I paused. "Paul, excuse me. This burger has an egg on it, and I said West has an egg allergy."

Paul looked flustered and worried. "I know ma'am, but when I tried to tell you, you said 'I know.'"

Ah! Dammit! C'mon, Christine!

"I'm sorry, don't worry about it. Would you mind just taking this back, and I'll pay for it–" Before I finished the sentence, West had leaned over his high chair, his pudgy fingers grabbing the egg.

"NO WEST, NO!" I screamed in the middle of the restaurant. Maya looked scared. I couldn't get the egg out of West's mouth quick enough. He'd swallowed it.

I snapped. *How could you let this happen? What is wrong with you? Why aren't you controlling the situation?* Even though I knew West swallowed just a piece of the egg, I kept opening his mouth as I tried to stick my fingers down his throat. Others were looking at us, their eyes wondering if I was abusing my child.

"He has an egg allergy! " I clarified. "I'm trying to stop him from getting sick and throwing up!" Tears started to fill my eyes, and I started feeling short of breath. My chest throbbed. "I'm trying!" I yelled. "I'm trying!"

"I tried!" I cried, my hands covering my face.

You're a very successful woman. But you may have to step away from the logic and get to the emotional. The real. Logic has a way of helping us move past emotions, full steam ahead.

CHAPTER SIX

DROP OFF THE F***ING BURDENS AND BE GONE

H*ONNNNNKKK!* The car horn of the driver behind me yanks me back into the present.

"REALLY?! For one inch?" I yelled.

The kids and I were stuck in beltway traffic, headed to Aunt Lisa's. I planned to drop them off before I headed to an awards ceremony. I'd been nominated as one of the top 40 professionals under 40 years old in Baltimore. And a moment before Mr. Honks-A-Lot showed his talent, I had just heard a commercial for the 26th Annual Champions of Courage Essay Competition on the radio.

"HA!" I chuckle, "the irony of hearing this conversation on today of all days."

My mind had wandered back to the time I told my grandparents about my entry...and the time I attempted to tell my mom as well. I remember reading the announcement for the Champions of Courage Essay Competition while I was in my school library. I immediately decided to apply:

Twenty Baltimore area students will appear on TV saluting their personal heroes this February for the 10th annual "Champions of Courage" Black History Month Essay Competition. Each student will also be honored at a Gala Awards Program and will receive a $50 award. The competition challenges high school students to write a brief essay saluting their personal "Champion of Courage" as a positive role model who has touched their lives by sharing the teachings of Dr. Martin Luther King, Jr.

"$50?! Bitcchhh.... I'm going to knock this out the park."

(Fifty dollars can't even buy you a decent dinner for two these days, but back in 2002 when I was 16 years old and only making $7 an hour, that was Big Pimpin' type figures, son.)

Two years prior, I'd competed in my first state beauty pageant. I learned two things from that unholy experience: 1) It doesn't pay to be an introvert when you have to smile in a wedding ball gown for two hours straight; and 2) In competitions, you don't need to be the brightest. You don't need to be the prettiest. But you gotta be the cleverest.

I copied the announcement on a piece of loose-leaf paper and circled vital phrases: "personal heroes," "Dr. Martin Luther King, Jr.," and "role model." After a few minutes of brainstorming, I read between the lines and figured out my angle.

So basically, I theorized, I gotta name drop—the bigger, the better. Who's a black person or family member who's done something in the city that's got a ton of good publicity?

I had determined how to be noticed by the judges of the essay competition, but to make my piece really stand out, it needed to feature the thing most important to me: uplifting black women. (Yes, I've always been a feminist and very pro-black.)

I wrote out a few names and decided on one significant black woman in my family.

"Aunt Carol!" I exclaimed. My classmates looked up at me with confusion.

Aunt Carol was the first female—and first African American—superintendent of Anne Arundel County Public Schools in the county history. She'd obtained a master's degree in school administration with advanced studies in guidance and counseling from Johns Hopkins University. Additionally, she had earned a Doctor of Education from the University of Maryland. She'd received many accolades over the years, including the 1996 Maryland Superintendent of the Year, the Martin Luther King Peacemaker Award, and the Kathleen Kennedy Townsend Award for Excellence to Outstanding Maryland Women in Government Service. And, lastly, she had a damn building named after her...the Anne Arundel County Board of Education building.

She was gonna help me show everyone how successful black women from Baltimore can be, and she was going to get me my $50! Win-win.

I started crafting the outline for the essay, setting a reminder on my Nokia to call my Aunt Carol once I got to my grandmother's house.

I told my grandparents after school that I planned on writing an essay for the Champion of Courage competition. They were watching the news at the time, and coincidentally, a commercial for the competition had appeared on the TV, which made them even more excited.

"That's it right there," I said.

"My angel is gonna be on TV; I know it. This is your moment to shine." My grandmother Edna smiled, her eyes squinting and beaming with pride.

Chapter Six
Drop Off The F***ing Burdens and Be Gone

"HEY NOW!" my grandfather William (Willie for short) yelled as if he were currently watching my segment on TV. "Who you goin' write about, *Moi?*" He joked.

"I'm gonna write about Aunt Carol, I think."

I wasn't surprised they were already proud of me, even before I'd accomplished anything. They were more than grandparents—they were my biggest cheerleaders. Whether I was shaving my legs or graduating from middle school, they acted as if I was the first, the best and brightest, to have ever achieved the accomplishment. When I was embarrassed at school for skipping a grade and reading at a level higher than my classmates, my grandfather bought me an Encyclopedia Britannica set. He told me never to dull my shine to appease others. On the summer days, I was a shy, overweight 10-year-old girl riding the bus to literature camp. My grandmother would ask me to read her whatever story I'd completed that day and beamed with pride when I was done.

I spent most of my time with my grandparents since my parents divorced before I turned one. I lived with my mother, but she needed to work multiple jobs to make ends meet. It didn't take long for my grandparents to step in and help raise me. For a while, my mother and I even lived with them.

My grandfather Willie was a very tall man (at least 6'3") and stayed somewhat in shape throughout his life. I say somewhat because he never met a can of Budweiser he didn't like. In fact, his grandchildren knew they were becoming one of the "older grandkids" when he snuck them a sip of his beer on the porch on summer evenings. He loved to sing blues off-key and is the reason I have an appreciation for the Blues myself. It wasn't even until I was a teenager that he allowed me to listen to R&B and rap music in his Cadillac. His deep, raspy voice and brief conversations made him frightening to some but respected by all. But without a doubt, my favorite quality of my grandfather was his fluent cursing. In fact, for the 87 years he lived on this planet, I'd never had a conversation with him that didn't involve a curse word. Hell, he could curse while reading the grocery list.

Chapter Six
Drop Off The F***ing Burdens and Be Gone

That's not an exaggeration—because he was also cheap. Willie often cursed at the costly items my grandmother would put on the list.

"Shrimp for $39.99?" He'd fuss. "Edna, why the fuck you need this shit!"

But after his long stream of obscenities, he'd slam the front door, stroll to his Cadillac while jingling his keys, get in the car and drive to the grocery store to buy the shrimp. Because of Willie, cursing to me is as natural as the air I breathe. And for those who consider my cursing uncivilized, 58% of all women swear at someone or something EVERY DAY.

My grandmother Edna, or Granny, wasn't an inch past five feet tall. When she stood next to my grandfather, he was so tall and lanky, and she so short and curvy, they looked like the black Bert and Ernie. Granny was so short when she sat in chairs while wearing heels that she'd cross her legs and point her toes to the floor, trying to hide the fact her feet couldn't actually touch it. She had enough boobs to please eight women and entertain 24 men. She was responsible, trustworthy, and most importantly, gracious. She loved to cook and entertain family and friends. In fact, during the summer, she hosted so many people in her home every day that she simply started leaving her front door open instead of running back and forth to answer it all day long.

Like her husband, Granny cursed as well, but it was pretty infrequent. She most often preferred to get her point across while speaking slowly, ending her thoughts with a soft chuckle, pursed lips, and glassy eyes. I loved spending time with her. Though not a career woman, Edna WAS an exemplary role model, committed to the advancement of her downtown Baltimore neighborhood. She was devoted to the needs of her family and obsessed with both her grandchildren and her husband. Granny respected my individuality. We were both comfortable being candid with one another. No matter what, she made me feel loved and comfortable in my own skin. I didn't feel as though I disrespected her if I cursed when we played spades (best

Chapter Six
Drop Off The F***ing Burdens and Be Gone

partner ever, by the way). I was disciplined; I knew there was a line between being respectful and playful, and I never crossed that line.

Our most enduring tradition was watching The Oprah Winfrey Show. Every year we promised each other we'd figure out a way to attend next year's taping, but unfortunately, we never did. Eleven years later, as best friends, my grandparents would both leave this world just months within each other.

During the same afternoon that we were talking about the Champions of Courage Essay Competition, my grandmother told me my mother was picking me up and taking me home for dinner.

Uninterested in the news, I replied, "Okay."

An hour later, the house phone rang, and Willie answered. "Yellow!"

"I'm outside!" I could hear my mother shout from the receiver.

I nodded to my grandfather that I'd heard her summon me. I mumbled goodbye to my grandparents, hugging my grandmother.

She comforted me, "Remember who loves you most."

I jogged out the door to my mom's Chevy Blazer, hopping in the passenger seat.

"How was school?" she inquired in an exhausted tone.

"Good. You know the Champions of Courage Competition on TV? I decided I'm gonna—"

"Have you decided who is going to be your debutante date?" she interrupted. Her eyes were fixed straight ahead on the road, but her abrupt, decisive tone gave the impression she was reading from a mental checklist.

"No," I answered. I didn't even bother to finish my sentence. It was clear she was in a rush, most likely moving from one item on her checklist to the next. It would be a big mistake to interrupt my mother Marsha's run of show (also called life).

I know it's cliché to say this, but if you looked up "momboss" in the dictionary (if it were actually in the dictionary), you'd see the picture of my mother, Marsha J. Parham. Well...maybe the thesaurus. She is pretty damn close. She's stunningly gorgeous, but She. Commands. Rooms. She's persuasive by nature but never afraid of confrontation. If a challenge arises, Marsha's more likely to remove a threat than remove herself *from* it.

The woman is highly educated, having obtained one bachelor's degree and TWO master's degrees in leadership and management. She's always been the "manager of" this, "the director of" that. I mean, shit; I could stop there. But pieces of paper don't make you a "momboss." Six-inch heels, baby. She grinds from Monday to Friday and works from Friday to Sunday. As a single mom, she put two kids through some of the best private schools in Baltimore while working two full-time jobs. She approaches business and life in a logical fashion: analyzing situations, checking facts, referring to previous related incidents, and then arriving at a sensible course of action.

But her major fault was the complete and utter absence of owning her shit in every aspect of her life. As a mother, she had no patience for indecisiveness or ignorance. (And I don't know if you've met many kids, but when it comes to those qualities, their cup runneth over, because they haven't learned everything they need to know in the world!) When she said she was going to get something done, come hell or high water, she did it. But because Marsha put those same expectations on her children, she misidentified their mistakes as laziness and dishonesty.

For all her professional accomplishments and her corporate reputation, neither was worth a damn at home, behind closed doors, or in the heart of her daughter. Marsha was polished and perfect in a boardroom, choosing every word carefully. She emphasized the importance of manners and was polite to strangers, young and old. But at home... ugh.

Chapter Six
Drop Off The F***ing Burdens and Be Gone

I remember one Mother's Day we were coming home from celebrating the day with my grandmother. I'd saved up the money given to me from birthdays, Christmas, and chores to purchase Marsha, a foot spa. I was carrying it from the Blazer to the house:

"Aunt Lisa told me one time you, her, and Uncle David were smoking weed on the church steps," I laughed. My aunt had told me this during the party not to portray my mother in a bad light, but to show a human side of her.

"I never did that," Marsha snapped, walking quickly in front of me. "That was your aunt and uncle. Not me." She spoke in a defensive, direct tone as though I was a reporter with a tape recorder, and she was a member of the Trump Administration.

I kept laughing. "It was just a comment—"

The box for the foot spa was so hefty I couldn't see while I was walking, and so I tripped on a branch from a tree above us, dropping the box. I immediately picked it up, but even though the foot spa didn't break, it was too late. She'd already heard it drop and immediately saw red.

She started to scream in my face. "WHY CAN'T I HAVE NICE THINGS?! THIS IS SUPPOSED TO BE A DAY FOR ME!"

I was terrified to move, let alone speak. My ten-year-old body felt frozen and paralyzed in the middle of the street. I had one job that day, which was to make my mother cheerful on Mother's Day, and I had failed. Little did I know I'd continue to fail at it every year for the next 21 years (and counting). Marsha always made me feel as if I was the burden in her life, the consolation prize she was forced to accept after losing the game show called marriage.

I vowed to be a different kind of mother when I came of age. Kids don't ask to be here and don't deserve to be raised as if you're doing them a favor. *If I gotta do it like my mom and affect someone else's life*, I used to think, *this is my chance to do it perfectly.*

Chapter Six
Drop Off The F***ing Burdens and Be Gone

I'm sure living up to being her mom, or at least the image of her mom in my eyes was quite difficult. Our dynamic was very different from that between my grandmother and me. (I talked about sex all the time with my grandmother, and yet I'm still waiting for 'the sex talk" from my mom. At this point, I'm 31 years old with two kids.) My mother assumed she was smarter than me because she was older. She didn't apologize to me when she was wrong, and she didn't listen.

Marsha's house was less than a mile from my grandparent's home, and in minutes, we'd arrived. I noticed she pulled up to the front door as opposed to parking.

"I gotta run a few errands, but you go inside and have dinner. It's in the fridge."

I barely closed the car door before I saw her check her PalmPilot, throw it in her Coach bag, and start to reverse down the one-way street. She put the SUV in drive, driving down a side street. With that, she'd dropped off her burden. She was gone.

Well, what the fuck? I ranted, standing in the street, my monogrammed red L.L. Bean backpack on the pavement.

I just left fresh fried chicken, green beans, and potato cakes for this?

Chapter Six
Drop Off The F***ing Burdens and Be Gone

For all her professional accomplishments and her corporate reputation, neither was worth a damn at home, behind closed doors, or in the heart of her daughter.

Chapter Seven

F***ING AJ HERBERT

I t's time for morning medicines," I yelled into the hall from the kids' bathroom.

Maya rushed into the hallway from her room and into the bathroom. "I'm ready, Mommy!"

West peeked his head from his bedroom.

"I'll come to you, buddy, one second," I sighed.

I gave Maya her Zyrtec, Flonase, Singulair, multivitamin, and inhaler. She was devoid of energy or interest in the task the entire way through. My inappropriate scene—I can't bring myself to call it a breakdown—in the middle of a fucking Red Robin back in January had left me embarrassed. My kids were STILL scared I might scream, laugh, or cry at any minute.

"Mommy, do you know what time *The Descendants* is coming on TV today?" Maya asked.

"I don't know." I moaned.

"Can I have strawberry syrup with my pancakes this morning?" She continued.

I exhaled.

"I promise I'll eat it..."

"I don't care, Maya," I replied to her.

Maya looked at me, puzzled, but only for a millisecond. She still was, in fact, a child who'd just been told she could eat pancakes with strawberry syrup. She wasn't questioning that shit. Maya skipped back to her bedroom.

I put everything away in the medicine cabinet, heading to the stairs to start breakfast. After locking the childproof gate, I realized I hadn't given West his medicine. The six-foot walk to his room seemed like a task too heavy to bear for my weak legs. I turned around on the step and headed downstairs.

I don't care. I'll do it later, I thought.

"Hey, babe!" I heard James yell from the family room. After being released from the hospital, he decided to make a few life changes, starting with making an effort to stay out of the basement.

He'd started a new job, fully believing the stress of his former accounting position had gotten to him. He was even seriously considering taking a permanent vacation from the world of accounting, and I supported it. And he'd been trying to pay more attention to me and the kids and chores around the home.

But even though I'd noticed his small changes, I didn't care. But I was beyond exhausted. I'd reached a state of giving less than three fucks about my entire world. We'd had a screaming match when he returned from the hospital, so I suppose in these months we had nowhere to go but up. Ultimatums were given ("if you don't stop this fucking drinking, then I'm taking the kids!"). Lifestyles were questioned ("That damn job of yours with those good ole boys is stressing you out!"). History was brought up ("When I wanted to leave you when we were engaged, you said if I married you, you'd stop drinking!"), and divorce was threatened.

"Yes, James." I asked flatly.

"Are you going to the gym this morning?" James questioned.

"No. I have to lead a global conference call, so I gotta hop on in... oh, shit. Three minutes ago." I shrugged and went to the kitchen table, powering up my laptop. After logging onto my computer, Office confirmed that I was now five minutes late for the call. I joined the Skype meeting.

"Hi, everyone. I apologize for joining late. Who do we already have on?"

"Hi, Christine. This is Yvonne from Peru, Olivia from Australia, and William from London. No worries about joining late, but..." I could hear the hesitation in Yvonne's voice.

"...do you need a minute?"

I glanced at the corner of the laptop screen to see my face was being projected in the meeting. I'd forgotten to turn off the video feature.

My eyes were red, with puffy bags underneath them. My lips were crusty, and dried drool was cracking out the corner of my mouth. My once tightly coiled hair was dehydrated, frizzy, and packed onto my head.

Looking back at me was a hollow, depressed shell.

I turned off the video feature, and my default image—a carefully curated picture of me with a long chestnut wig and smoky eye makeup appeared. That's better—the image of me I wanted my colleagues to see. "No, I'm fine. Let's jump right in."

"Hi, Christine. It's Katie from Moms Incorporated. We're on the line and ready to jump into our deck. Do you want to drive, or should

Chapter Seven
F***ing AJ Herbert

we?" Katie was the CEO of an organization that provided insights on millennial mom consumers for big companies, helping them to understand the needs, wants, and concerns of today's mother. I'd met her at a conference and thought she could be an excellent external resource to drive home some of the points I'd been trying to beat into my colleagues for months now.

"I don't care. You can go," I replied. Just then, West started screaming from the top of the stairs.

"Mooooommmmmmmyyyy!   Mooooommmmmmmyyyy! MAAAWWWWWMMMMAAAAYYY!"

"I apologize, guys. I was just about to hit the mute button. Couldn't get to it in time."

"No worries, Christine," Olivia replied, coming off mute. "It's bedtime here, and I'm dealing with the same issue. Working mom problems, right?" Olivia chuckled.

Katie chimed in. "Yeah, how fitting of us to be running through this deck! Great tee up, Christine. We all go through this."

Somehow, that felt comforting in my drained state. I half smiled to myself and went back on mute. "James, can you see what West wants?" I yelled around into the family room.

I looked at the clock: 7:09 a.m. *Jesus. And I got at least 10 more hours of work?* I groaned. The irony of me sitting on this kitchen stool, listening to what other mothers want and need, and trying to solve their problems—as if I've got all this shit figured out. How can I be my brother's keeper if I've lost my own got damn mind? We're just the blind leading the damn blind!

James came back down the stairs. "He just needed his pacifier, and it'd fallen behind something. Don't worry. I cleaned it off."

"I don't care," I replied.

Chapter Seven
F***ing AJ Herbert

I stared past my computer to a picture frame. My eyes adjusted to the picture of my grandmother and me. Right before she passed away, we'd taken the picture. Her smile had caused her plump cheeks to make her eyes squint. We were holding hands and had our heads tilted in the same direction. It sounds strange, but at that very moment, I knew how Simba felt when he started at the watering hole and saw Mufasa's reflection.

I exhaled deeply in shame. She was looking down on me from heaven. Was she proud of what she saw? Granny was my role model when it came to being a wife, mother, and woman. But compared to her, I feel like an imposter. I got everything in order? Shit. I don't have anything together; I'm struggling to stay afloat while not drowning in the pool of responsibility called marriage and parenting. Not only did she excel at that, but she had a social life! She never penciled in spending time with other people. Friends just stopped by, and she made time for them.

How the hell did she do it? I thought.

My mind came back to the presentation. Katie was sharing a slide about adulting. "...And even if you haven't heard this millennial term before, it basically means to be responsible, to tackle head-on. You're not only focusing on the logistical parts of your life you'd like to avoid but the abstract too."

Hmph, I scoffed. What's the point? It's not like it leads to happiness. I adulted and did everything I was supposed to do. I listened to the advice of others. I got married to someone I was best friends with. I had kids and raised them in a safe environment. And I still felt like I was a complete fucking mess.

The weekend had arrived, and with it, the crisp, fall air. The comforting weather served as a backdrop for a great Saturday with the kids, trick or treating for the Halloween weekend. James joined us for the walk around the neighborhood, even getting into the spirit with us by agreeing to dress in a family Halloween costume.

Chapter Seven
F***ing AJ Herbert

We were the black Incredibles, with cute little West serving as baby Jack Jack. We were giving all this melanin awesomeness to All Hallows Eve. Too bad the only ones to bear witness to our black fierceness were our neighbors' nannies. In our neighborhood, no homeowner actually came to the door. They were as crisp year-round to my family as the current fall air.

While Maya walked up to the last house, attempting to completely fill the second bucket of candy, James turned to me.

"I love you," he said.

I could feel it; it felt different this time. Perhaps it had been the combination of crying and sitting and staring for a week. I had felt depleted and drained from serving others, and so those three words felt real. Whatever it was, I needed to hear it the way he said it.

"I love you too," I smiled.

We headed back home and didn't even go into the house—we went straight to my SUV. We were going to a Halloween birthday party for my cousin Lindsey thrown by her husband, AJ.

"Woooo! That was so much fun! I got so much candy!" Maya screamed, unaware of the height of her voice. Yes, my miniature Ric Flair had already dug into her bucket and was off to the moon.

I just chuckled. "Yeah, Maya, it was."

We arrived at the party twenty minutes later, and it was clear that though this was a house party, no expense was spared. The home I often visited was turned into a haunted house of wonder. Warm party trays full of chicken alfredo, buffalo wings, and chicken tenders were being served. Halloween-themed punch (a mix of fruit punch and Sprite) and a side table overflowing with Halloween candy was on display for the children. And a clean version of "Truth Hurts" by Lizzo was flowing from the Bluetooth fog machine.

"Wow, this is nice!" I turned to James, and we looked at each other in delight. Maya was already off to the races. She'd spotted her cousins across the room and was sharing with them all the candy she'd just hijacked from our neighbors.

"Don't y'all look cute?" Lindsey walked up to us from across the living room, giving each of us hugs and asking how we were. I shared a great deal with my cousin, and even if I hadn't told her about James' hospital visit, everyone in the family already knew.

"We're good," James replied, understanding the hidden meaning of the question. "I'm going to go find AJ."

"Happy birthday!" I yelled to Lindsey, giving her another hug. I was blessed to have many great friends and family members, but Lindsey was the only one who was a friend, mom, wife, and life goals.

Lindsey was undoubtedly a port in the motherhood storm. I often felt guilty for sharing my thoughts and feelings with her. As a wife and the mother of two young children herself, all my problems seemed trivial. It was unfair to confide in someone who could do nothing to better my situation (and who was just four years older than me). Still, it felt genuinely good to turn to someone who just...got it. I needed her.

Lindsey always looked polished. Her hands and toes were still perfectly gel-manicured, she always knew what the latest Korean beauty product was, and had uncovered the secret to barely-there, dewy makeup.

Looking at her smiling face reminded me of what she said to me as my bridesmaid on my wedding day. She was applying my makeup in the hotel room bathroom when she gave me a piece of advice that I ignored.

"Remember; don't start something you can't finish. If you don't cook every day now, don't start doing it when you get married. Marriage doesn't magically solve problems, and it doesn't magically turn us into new women."

Chapter Seven
F***ing AJ Herbert

Looking back on that comment from my current fragile state, I realized I was drunk in love; a naïve dumbass. I had already been catering to James as his girlfriend and fiancé, so I thought it would be nothing to continue once I was married. And I thought it would be simple to do the same for the children we had because I was responsible and so full of love. Turns out, I didn't realize I was setting myself up for failure from the start.

Lindsey's husband, AJ, was headed to us with James behind him. I loved AJ, and I loved him for Lindsey. In fact, everyone loved AJ. Most women loved him because he was a tall, caramel-colored, muscular black man in his 40s. But I loved him because he was smart and he was family. He was also an attentive husband and father. He always seemed to proactively anticipate their needs, all while keeping a positive attitude.

"Everybody, I'd like to celebrate the birthday girl for one moment," AJ yelled over the music. A woman across the room turned down the music from an iPhone, and AJ continued.

"I just wanna thank y'all for coming out and celebrating Halloween with us, and for celebrating my wife's birthday. I love all of you here in the room, but I love this woman even more."

I turned to look at James, who I could see was avoiding eye contact with me. He stared to the floor, his head down while he bit his bottom lip and tapped his hand against the side of his thigh. At that moment, I could tell he was feeling inferior. AJ's "awesomeness" had bothered James in the past, and he, too, often compared their marriage to our own. We couldn't help it. Not only were AJ and Lindsey close to us in age, but they'd gotten married and had children around the same time. Hell, Maya, and my oldest nephew Evan were in the same daycare!

As usual, AJ knew exactly what to say to elevate his marriage... and unknowingly elevate my marital problems in my mind. *Ugh you, sweet son of a bitch,* I thought. AJ was surrounded by friends and family, and at that moment, he only saw his wife. I smiled and clapped along with everyone else.

"Aight now, everybody. Enjoy yourselves and the food I took all damn day to cook from the shit I saw on Pinterest!" AJ joked, and everybody laughed.

This dude is KILLING me, I yelled internally. Now he cooks, and from Pinterest recipes too?!

I was trying to pull myself out of my rut. I was having a great time thus far at the party; I, too, was surrounded by friends and family. Yet I'd never felt so alone in my damn life.

James snuck behind AJ while he continued with his speech. I grinned while James walked towards me. I gave him a bear hug, the side of my face deflating against the padding of his Mr. Incredible costume's chest.

I caught the woman who turned down the music out the corner of my eye as she was preparing three plates of food at the same time. With one barely balanced on her right forearm, she'd extended her hand with a second plate in it, scooping chicken alfredo onto the plate. The third plate was in her mouth. Her kids were by her side, offering no help in holding a plate. They were asking her to hurry, though, because they were hungry.

What the hell is she doing? I questioned. She looks like an idiot. One of the plates is gonna...

Sure enough, the plate she was struggling to balance on her arm fell. I saw a man, her husband, I assumed, look at her drop the plate. In fact, I realized he'd been watching her the whole time.

Why didn't his ass jump in and help her before the plate fell? Then I counted again the plates she was making, jumping to an assumption. Shit, why didn't he get his own got damn plate?

Chapter Seven
F***ing AJ Herbert

I closed my eyes, buried my face deeper into James' chest, and breathed deeply.

"I told you how you hurt me...you don't care

Now I'm crying and deserted...Ain't nobody tell me this is love

When you're immune to all my pain..."

James was exhausted from all the day's activities and slept in the car on the ride home from the party. I sang Beyoncé, keeping myself entertained while his face was pressed against the passenger side window snoring.

My phone chimed from a text notification. WOMANIZER.

"I enjoyed our conversation a few weeks ago. Have I done something to upset you since?" the text read.

I waited until I stopped at a red light and replied. "No, but I'm dealing with a lot and can't be bothered right now." I put my phone back in my purse. It did feel satisfying confiding in someone who knew me; someone with whom I had once had a romantic relationship. He'd always understood my drivers and how my past and my relationship with my mother caused me to behave in specific ways in situations. I didn't need to explain my actions, my passions, and my fears with him; he just got it. We clicked.

But there's a reason your exes are your exes. And, at this point in my life, the last thing I needed was an ex-boyfriend fucking it up more. I knew where this was headed and where he was headed. I'd changed his name to WOMANIZER in my phone for a reason. He'd slither into my life, claiming to be a friend and confidant. I'd fallen for the trap before.

*I've been talking to this man...He's been saying what I like and...
he says sweet things in my ear...I needed to hear*

Ah, Jill; you hit me at my core every time, girl. I hear you, Ms. Scott. I guess God was trying to talk to me through the radio that night. I was spending too much time talking to everyone but the one person I should.

I pulled into our driveway and nudged James' arm. "James, wake up. We're home."

James grunted, slowly sitting up as he turned around to see Maya and West fast asleep. Carbon copies of their father, they too were leaned over and sleeping up against the car door. We grabbed the children, picked them up, and walked up to the driveway.

"After we put the kids down," I whispered, "can I talk to you?"

"Yeah," he said, concerned.

"I don't want to fight," I reassured him. "We're in a good place. I just want to talk."

James disarmed the alarm system and carried Maya up to her room. I followed with West, putting him on his toddler bed. I gave my baby boy three soft kisses on his cheek and watched his eyes twitch.

I closed his door and met James in the hall. We decided to have a conversation in our bedroom. We changed out of our costumes, and I put my Mrs. Incredible wig on the dresser. I put on my nightshirt, James' old high school t-shirt, and sat on the side of the bed.

"James, where did you go when you disappeared from the party for a half-hour?" I was afraid of the answer.

James finished putting on his track pants but didn't turn to me to answer the question. "I went outside in the backyard to get some fresh air."

Chapter Seven
F***ing AJ Herbert

"Did you drink while you were out there?" My voice trembled. The fear of having my husband spend another week in the hospital from another alcohol-induced seizure made my blood turn cold.

"Yeah," he sniffed while answering, his body slightly off-balance. "I know what I said. I'm working on myself, but as the man of the house, I have a lot of stress," James responded flatly. That was some old school bullshit from that outdated father of his. It broke my heart whenever James quoted him. James was smarter than that, and he was taking the easy way out.

"I know you have a lot of stress. What do you think I have? I'm trying to grow and evolve and be better, but I can't compromise on this. I can't compromise on you working on you. Your growth can look different from mine, but you need to grow."

I thought for a moment, and the silence in the room scared me. It was solemn, almost as though death had entered the room. "I don't know what happened to us. I mean, I know marriages go through good and bad times. And I know everyone has their demons. But this isn't about the drinking. It's more than that."

"Marriage is like a car, you know that." He'd given me that metaphor before, no doubt something he'd picked up from some TV show. "When they're new, you're less likely to experience issues. But the minute you've settled into it as parents and the oil change light comes on, you worry."

"Yeah, that's it. I'm worried," I answered.

"We just need some maintenance," he replied.

"If we're a car, we're breaking down from neglect," I said, my head sinking into my chest. We'd both never taken the metaphor this far in conversation. "We've tried marriage counseling; I'm in counseling. What if this is it? What if the car is about to die?"

James just stared at the window. He couldn't see anything but his reflection, as the sun had long gone down. I guess he was seeing what

Chapter Seven
F***ing AJ Herbert

I saw in him on the hospital bed; the same image I'd seen of myself on my computer laptop: the loss of hope. The loss of joy. Misery.

I continued. "It's not like this escalated quickly. We've been brushing things under the rug and living different lives. Why are we fighting so hard to keep this car alive?" I couldn't bring myself to say marriage. "I keep saying 'it will get better when...,' but I don't know how to finish that sentence."

"What do you mean?" he retorted. "We're in it for the kids!"

"And what are we going to do when the kids are older?" I interrupted.

"We both wanted to have a loving mom and dad in the house, and if you divorce me, the kids won't have that. They'll just have a dad in one house and a busy working mom in another."

At that moment, James picked up a gun and shot me in the heart. At least that's what it felt like. Being a present wife and mother meant everything to me. I wanted so badly to let love guide my tender heart through the fog. I wanted to do what my grandmother did, and my own always-busy, stressed-out mother couldn't. If we did divorce, it wasn't because I was craving a single life. I wasn't looking for an escape, but I couldn't deny I was a prisoner in my current world.

I had to accept that it may be what I needed.

"EXACTLY! Loving! Does this feel like love to you? You want to raise them in a house like the one you grew up in? And why did you have to say busy working mom? Why can't I just be a mom?" my voice trembled. "I work, and I work hard, but it's because I love you. I want you to have everything in this world! I want our daughter to see a strong woman! I want our kids to have everything in this world!"

At this point, the tears broke free from my eyes. I let them fall down my cheeks. What was more important to me—my marriage or my way of doing things? Why did I have to defend my passion? Because it included being validated and recognized outside of these four walls? Why couldn't I just crack the code? Why couldn't I be a great

Chapter Seven
F***ing AJ Herbert

mother, wife, and businesswoman? Why did I have to choose? And more importantly, why did I feel as if James was getting in the way of that?

"You. You. Your plan." James hissed as if he could hear the questions in my head. "You have everything in control and know what should happen next. It's as if the kids and I can't fit into your plan. We're not meeting your expectations, and something's wrong with us. We're human, Christine."

He continued. "Jesus. It's just not fun anymore. You're not fun anymore."

I fumed. "Do you wanna know why I'm not fun anymore? I don't have TIME to BE fun! I'm too busy providing and protecting. I'm making sure you don't have seizures or that the kids are taking their medicine! I'm tired of being the only adult in the house! I'm tired of being the one making sacrifices! Sometimes, I feel like you're holding me back. Sometimes I just...I just wish...you'd get...out of my way."

I'd gone too far.

"I'll get out of your way. Go be happy. Date. You've done it once when we were married already, right?" James snapped. A shameful WOMANIZER dig that literally made me clutch my fists as I pressed them against my chest.

This discussion was getting off track. We started discussing our marriage and James' drinking. Somehow, it turned into what was wrong with me. But I wasn't the problem.

Was I?

Maybe he was right. Maybe James wasn't killing the relationship. Maybe it was the both of us. After all, my abilities don't lie in being able to change James. They only lied in being able to change me.

There we sat, two people with strong work ethics on the brink of divorce. We were educated in everything but how to love and be married.

Moments passed. We sat in the room in silence. James got up from the bed.

"I'm going down to the basement," he mumbled with his back to me.

As I heard him walk down the stairs, I let my body fall to the side on my pillow, and let the tears flow freely.

"Remember; don't start something you can't finish. If you don't cook every day now, don't start doing it when you get married. Marriage doesn't magically solve problems, and it doesn't magically turn us into new women."

CHAPTER EIGHT

ROME TOOK HOW F***ING LONG?

"M ommy...are you angry today?" Maya whispered. She stood over my body as I woke up that morning on the floor. Her dazzling bright eyes were staring at me, full of fear and concern.

Nearly a month had passed since James decided to move out and stay with his parents. Every day I progressed through the same emotions: anger in the morning, numbness in the afternoon, and sorrow in the evening.

Having my daughter ask me that question broke my heart, but Maya was wiser than some thirtysomething-year-olds. Me in particular. I'd just spent all night as I had for the past 22 days—crying uncontrollably while trying to control the uncomfortable pressure and pain in my chest every 15 minutes. There I lay for seven hours, unable to lift my body from the hardwood floor. I was lightheaded and short of breath.

Just yesterday, I'd attempted a family outing (sans James), deciding to take the kids to a matinee showing of *Smallfoot*. Finally, I thought. It was an activity with the kids where no one would notice their father wasn't around. For two hours, no one stared at the poor black woman, all alone with her young child and baby. I didn't catch the judgmental glances.

After the movie, Maya walked back to the concession stand. "Mommy, can I have some more popcorn?"

"No, Maya. You've had enough," I responded quickly.

"But why not?"

"Because I have to save money," I said, frustrated with myself for explaining my actions to a child.

"Hmph!" Maya stomped her right foot and refused to move.

"YOU BETTER MOVE YOUR ASS!" I yelled. I'd lost my temper, and the stares immediately resumed. But the look on the other parents' faces weren't ones of concern for me. Instead, they were concerned for my children.

I knew if I couldn't make Maya move from the concession stand, I was about to see some woman take her cell phone from her purse, calling the cops on me for parenting while black.

"Where is your daddy? Why are you giving me grief? I just took you to the movies. Where is he? Did he take you? Has he even called you?" I continued.

Maya was right to be concerned about me that morning because I was taking all my anger out on the very people who didn't deserve it—my babies. I'd lost interest in singing to every ouchie and hearing about what happened during nap time.

I was just so furious. James was a die-hard basketball fan. When we were dating, he'd smile and whisper in my ear that our marriage was going to be like a championship. Each time I was pregnant, he'd rub my stomach and talk into my belly button. "We're adding team members," he'd say. Fast forward to today, and I felt as if our team had fallen apart. Our coach had abandoned us.

"Can I play with my iPad?" Maya asked, bringing me out of my head.

"Sure, baby, but please be nice to Siri."

Maya stared at me as if she was saying, "Bitch, you know Siri isn't real." But it wasn't about that. I got so sick of hearing her bark orders, yelling and grunting and getting frustrated with the iPad when it wouldn't download an app, or search YouTube Kids fast enough for her. She was treating that damn pink silicone-covered thing like it was her slave.

Maya grabbed my hand as if to help me lift my body from the bed. I huffed and then sat up. "Mommy, do you have to work today?"

"Naw, baby," I yawned, smacking my mouth around like a horse.

"Good," she grinned. "I like to spend time with you on Saturdays. I don't like when you do work on the weekend."

I nodded.

"I'm gonna go play ABCMouse," Maya exclaimed as she skipped off to find her iPad. That damn app. Their commercials make it seem like ABCMouse can help former high school dropouts connect with their kids, solve inner-city educational issues, and even accelerate brain growth in kids who were in the NICU.

Yeah, ok, ABCmouse.com. Since you're so busy working miracles, why don't you do something to keep my kids in their own damn rooms until 7 a.m. on Sunday mornings?

I sighed and stared at the ceiling fan.

The next morning, after another solo attempt of my already complicated morning routine, I headed to Starbucks to meet a colleague before work. Zara Green was a personal growth and relationship coach I'd met a few years prior. We'd planned to get together months ago when she was in Baltimore. I wanted to write an article about the work she and her husband Alfred Edmond Jr. (all-

Chapter Eight
Rome Took How F***ing Long?

around badass and senior vice president and executive editor-at-large of *Black Enterprise*) were doing with their platform, The Grown Zone.

This woman is a genius, I thought. Her private coaching could help so many of my readers sort through a myriad of relationship challenges and crisis situations, I thought.

Ha! Little did I know I was gonna need her more than anyone! Well, shit, I added. I'm just gonna make the most of this meeting while I slip a few questions in about me and my situationship.

It was easy to spot Zara by her short cinnamon-colored curls across the café. Plus, it didn't hurt that we were the only two black women in the place.

"Mrs. ZARA GREEEEEEEN!" I sang.

"Christine?" she questioned, a smile slowly appearing on her face. "What a pleasure it is to meet you in person!" Zara stood, and we hugged as if we'd known one another for years.

"I'm so excited and happy to meet you and can't wait to get started. Have you ordered?"

"Yes, I have," Zara said. "Go ahead and order."

I put my laptop bag, purse, and coat over the chair across from Zara and walked to the counter.

"What can I get started for you?" the barista asked.

"I'll take a grande cinnamon dolce latte, please; thank you," I requested. This separation had me so over being fit and healthy that I'd gone full crack(er barrel) head. I was overindulging every moment I got. It was undoubtedly showing too. I'd worn a full dress to the Starbucks that day because it was the only thing I owned that didn't show my new rolls.

A few moments later, Zara and I were sipping our drinks, laughing and talking like old friends. Though we'd only connected online before, I genuinely liked Zara's spirit and trusted she gave married couples solid advice. She was older and wiser but didn't fall back on that to qualify her expertise. Zara was an author, speaker, and a realist. She'd been married before and been divorced previously.

"Zara, let's get into it," I said, wrapping up our previous conversation. I took out my iPhone from my handbag, dropping it on the floor.

"Do you need help?" Zara asked.

"Nope, I'm good," I replied. I leaned over, putting my iPhone on the table so I could start recording our conversation.

"My goodness. You mean business," Zara chuckled. "Girl, you are so tightly wound that you are gonna snap!" She laughed. "I'm just messing with you. What if we just have a casual conversation? You must be a big planner, huh?"

I felt so seen! What the..."Yeah, I am, I'm sorry," I dismissed. "Have you done a Meyers-Briggs test?"

Zara nodded.

"I'm an ISTJ, so I believe in clear guidelines, rules, and am always by the book," I stated.

"Huh, but on the other hand, doesn't that also make you often stubborn, insensitive, and too judgmental of yourself and others?" she responded.

Oop! Okay, Mrs. Green. Get me all the way together! I moved the iPhone from the table and stuttered, "I'm fully aware that people either love me or hate me, but no one is in a gray area."

Zara laughed. "So, what do you want to talk about for the article?"

Fuck it. "You know what? Let's discuss what it means to be a wife and mother in today's world. Sometimes I feel like social media has

Chapter Eight
Rome Took How F***ing Long?

ruined our society. Everyone's trying to portray a perfect life that others should aspire to. But life is hard."

I continued rambling, "It's like you're a bad wife if you excel at work and a bad mother if you're concerned with your own happiness. Why are we so quickly judged as selfish, but men are leaders when they do the same things?"

Zara smiled at me, giving me that older black woman, "I SEE you and KNOW why you're asking me these things" smile. She paused, saying,

"Most people who get married have constructs in their minds of how marriage will be post 'I Do.' But at The Grown Zone, we try to do relationships that are based on honor, esteem, and respect. That is the only thing that's a sustainable foundation for any relationship. Otherwise, somebody is going to be unhappy. As a result, that marriage breaks down and crumbles. The more you lay on top of it, the more unstable that foundation is going to be."

I listened attentively, praying my mom brain allowed me to remember everything this genius was saying later. Zara continued:

"The more we learn and grow, the more our capacity to love increases. You have to be willing to do what's necessary as the relationship changes. As long as there are honor, esteem, and respect in the relationship, you can give each other the space you need to grow. You've got to have the mentality that, when you hit something you have not experienced before, you don't get in your feelings, and you don't get jacked up by it. Instead, you go and get some training. There's something you need to learn. Any time you hit a brick wall, that's the universe saying, 'Boo, you need to learn a little bit more about this so you that you can apply what you need to apply to this.'"

I sat back in my chair and exhaled, addressing the elephant in the room. "Zara, I have to be honest with you. I'm going to put all of this in the article, but I asked you about this because I'm going through a separation right now."

Zara looked concerned. "I'm sorry to hear that."

"Thanks, but I'm taking it harder than I imagined. I feel as if my husband isn't interested in fighting for the marriage or for me. And I feel abandoned with my children. I thought I wouldn't miss or need him when we separated because I'd have everything in control. I thought he was the weak link in my life."

"You look so young," Zara said. "Can I ask when you got married?"

"When I just got in my twenties," I replied.

Zara nodded. "Do you think you're the same woman you were in your early twenties?"

I shook my head, staring at the top of my coffee cup.

"That's not a bad thing, Christine," Zara reassured me. "What matters is that you're totally in touch with what distinguishes you from everyone else. When you know yourself, you're less likely to lose yourself. Maybe you didn't know yourself in your early twenties. Maybe you're getting to know yourself now. But for a marriage to work, a couple must understand their individual temperaments: their thoughts, emotions, and behaviors. They must be confident in who they are individually and as a team."

A team. There goes that phrase again.

"You know, it's funny," I said, "I have a friend who separated from her husband, and I ran into her when I was out with my children. She seemed to be fine even though she was living life without her husband. I saw on Facebook they recently reconciled. When I asked her what changed, she said he'd really fought for her, for the children and the marriage."

Zara listened.

"I just..." I stuttered, "Separation seemed like the solution to me. Like it would help me keep living life full steam ahead without the

Chapter Eight
Rome Took How F***ing Long?

'interruption' of my husband. Now I'm kind of just wondering why her marriage was worth the fight and mine is not."

Zara pulled her chair closer to mine and rubbed my back. She was right to do so because I wanted to cry but refused to in what was supposed to be a business meeting. "You're harping on the situation because it's so similar. But just because they felt their marriage was worth a damn doesn't mean if your marriage fails, you're not worth a damn."

I shrugged my shoulders. It was comforting to have someone to just listen to my issues instead of trying to solve them. I'd encountered so many "poor you, single black mom" stares, it felt like all of Baltimore thought they were gonna catch my separation cooties.

Zara asked, "Have you connected with any friends outside of the one who reconciled with her husband?"

I shook my head and sat up, remembering I was in a meeting. "No, I haven't."

"I think you should. Allow yourself to be more vulnerable."

"I'm pretty fucking vulnerable right now," I joked. We laughed at my inappropriate cursing. "No, I haven't been able to be that easily vulnerable since my grandmother passed away."

Zara listened, and I continued. "I remember when my grandfather died, just a few months before her. I drove to her house to see how she was doing. We were all alone, and I'd never seen her cry in sadness. She just kept repeating, 'How will I live without him? What am I going to do now?' It was then that I learned what sorrow and devotion truly were. I find myself now questioning if I feel grief and dedication for my husband—"

Zara finished my thought. "Or devotion to who you have become since getting married, and sorrow for the loss of that woman if you stay married."

"Exactly."

I sipped the coffee and stared through the glass door. I was torn.

On the one hand, I felt like the world was telling me to be a badass wife and mother while fighting for my rights and a seat at the table. On the other hand, I was being told to preserve my marriage at all costs and upkeep traditional family values. How the hell was I supposed to do both at the same time? More importantly, how was I supposed to do it alone? Didn't holding onto those outdated notions of motherhood, marriage, and career make so many older women feel unhappy, isolated, and insane? So what effect does the world think they will have on me?

I'm supposed to act as if I'm not dealing with more pressures than previous generations, and believe like those previous generations that traditional family values and eventual financial wealth will make me happy.

Fuck that.

False.

I'm fed up with being insane – doing the same thing over and over while expecting different results. I wanna do things differently.

A few days later, I'd asked Aunt Lisa to watch the kids a little longer so I could spend some time with my friends. They were still home for Thanksgiving break, and I was rarely able to get all of them together since they all lived in different cities. We'd been planning this happy hour for weeks now, and now with Zara's advice fresh in my mind, I was damned if I was gonna cancel that shit.

Friend get-togethers were for trash eating, reminiscing, and laughs. I was looking forward to all of that. I pulled into the parking space outside of T.G.I. Friday's full of energy for the first time in a long time. I found it hilarious that, although all of us had great jobs and

Chapter Eight
Rome Took How F***ing Long?

could afford to go to some swanky, upscale Maryland bar, we still chose to hang out at the same restaurant we ate at as teenagers.

These days, I was being invited out more frequently by close friends and family; but between work and the kids, I always had a convenient excuse not to go. It wasn't like I was that busy. I was blowing off a lot of my responsibilities to just stay in bed, fighting anxiety attacks.

Ever punctual, I arrived at 7:40. After all, to be on time is to be late. We were talking about black people here, so I knew these fools were all gonna come at 8:20, 20 minutes past when we agreed we'd meet up.

The waitress walked me to a booth near the window, and I plopped on the red leather seat. I kept plopping and sliding, plopping, and sliding to the middle of the booth. She walked away and there I sat, alone with the menus. Looking around, everyone was either paired up or with a group of friends. For the first time, I was alone. I was lonely. I knew I was meeting people just like everyone else but was this a feeling I'd be comfortable with for the rest of my life? Did I fuck with myself like that? Was I enough for me?

Just then, a knock on the glass window behind me took me out of my thoughts. I saw my brother, Christopher, and my sister, Jayia, standing outside the restaurant.

7:55? Oh, shit! These fools arrived on time!

"What up, bitches?" I screamed a little too loudly. A woman turned around and glared at me from her table. Eh, whatevs.

"Heyyyy," Jayia said, sweeping her blond wig du jour from her forehead. I loved Jayia. Though she was my third cousin (not my biological sister), my mom had practically adopted her in high school, and she'd become my confidant ever since. Jayia was the one and only person on Earth who knew where I'd buried all the bodies, and she never judged me for my decisions.

"Before you even say anything, I need to spend the night at the house tonight," Jayia stated in her feminine, yet raspy voice.

"That's fine," I replied, "but please put some clothes on. I hate when you sleep all ass out."

Jayia chuckled.

Christopher said, "I'm shocked. My niece and nephew let you have a night off!" He joked. My brother was six years younger than me, but through the course of this separation, he'd stepped into his 6'2" frame. Suddenly, he had turned into my big bro. He was there for every late-night call (when I swore I heard something other than the kids in the house), every TV I couldn't lift, and every car battery I couldn't start.

"I brought you something I think you could use." Christopher reached in his pocket and pulled out a clear packet of gummy worms.

"I wish!" I sighed. Those were clearly weed gummies, and I'd never smoked, drank, or eaten anything with weed in it. "But you know I can't do that."

"Why not?" Jayia sassed.

"That's what you need right now. You're way too uptight, prissy Chrissy!" Tee overheard the conversation while she walked to the table. I leaned up from the booth to give her a big hug, and, of course, I had to deliver a compliment.

"Where in the hell is your body? You look fabulous. I could snap your skinny tail in half!" I joked. She laughed as I pretended to fold her body in half.

The only thing worse for a food drug addict like me is finding another fiend with which you can bask in the unhealthy goodness. When I was in middle school, I met a vibrant, hilarious, and energetic classmate named Tiara (Tee for short). She grew to become one of my closest friends for over 20 years.

Chapter Eight
Rome Took How F***ing Long?

"Don't ignore what we talking about!" Tee observed me changing the subject. "Eat it!"

Christopher opened the packet and gave me three sugarcoated gummies.

"Did you guys know that more than half of adults have tried..."

Jayia interrupted my statistic. "Don't get started, marketing nerd. Just eat them!"

I laughed heartily. I took the gummies from my brother, chewing them to cheers and applause.

Seeing my squad's faces had already given me an overwhelming wave of calm—with or without weed. I see their faces every day on Instagram, but social media had ruined us. With best friends, sometimes you really do just need to see them in person, or, at the very least, pick up a phone to hear how they're truly doing. Instagram and Facebook can have you thinking you're in touch with someone, and their lives are entirely different.

Some people argue we overshare on social media as a society. I don't think we're sharing at all. I was a separated woman and needed my friends more than ever. It felt good to confide in them in person, surrounded by people who supported my growth and welcomed my vibe.

A few minutes later, Maurice, Adam, and Kierra—the final members of my squad—arrived. We ordered drinks and appetizers, reminiscing about when Maurice had cornrows, when Adam had an old white Ford Taurus with maroon interior, and when Jayia would style everyone's hair for dances.

They were reminding me of who I was, every facet of me. How opinionated I was, how determined I was, and how sure of myself I was at just 16 years old. I wondered for a brief moment in-between the laughs how I found myself in my current marital predicament. Zara was right. They did give me what I needed—a good laugh—but I was even more confused. I thought I had all the answers at 16. I thought I had all the answers when I got married. I thought I knew the best way to overcome issues. Sit down and write out your problems, research what's been done before or what's recommended, and course correct.

But it wasn't working. The only thing all that planning and logic had done was make me excel in my career. But my marriage had fallen apart, and I was lashing out at my children.

Just then, the lights in the restaurant got super bright, and their voices muffled. Kierra, also the only other mother in the group, noticed my puzzled face.

"Oh, shit, here it is. I think the gummies y'all gave her earlier kicked in," she grinned. "We've got a 420 mom now!"

Adam, knowing me well, must have known the weed would make me even more contemplative than what was already in my nature to be. He also knew me well because, for a brief time, we were roommates after college. I say brief because having him invade my space drove my controlling ass insane.

"Quit." That was Adam's nickname for me, stolen from when I was younger. Christopher couldn't say "Chris," so he said "Quit" instead.

Adam continued, "Come with me to the bar for a second. I wanna see what the bartender can make special for me."

Adam and I walked through the restaurant and up to the bar. We both leaned on the bar, and he turned to me. "I don't want a drink. I just wanna see how you're doing."

"I'm..."

"If you say fine, I'll punch you in your throat." Got damn, Adam!

"I mean, I'm trying to deal!" I responded.

Chapter Eight
Rome Took How F***ing Long?

"You'll be fine," he reassured. "A woke woman is never a broke woman." Adam was so wise beyond his years, just like his goddaughter Maya. I swear that's where she got it. Both were full of short phrases and sentences that could just drive a point home and punch you in the gut at the same time.

"That's the thing, I'm not feeling very woke. I feel confused. And alone. And frustrated. And right now, high, I think."

"Rome wasn't built in a day. Took 767 years." Adam replied, confidently.

"For real?" I said. "Well, damn." We laughed, and I swear I hadn't heard anything so funny in my life.

"I don't want everyone to wonder what's taking us so long, but I just want to say...don't feel like you're alone. You have us. You put a lot into your marriage, but you were still just in your early twenties when you got married, and no one could tell you differently. You absolutely loved that man." Adam said.

"I love that man," I corrected. "Not loved."

Adam disregarded the comment, waving his muscular arm in the air. "Aight, aight; Love. But maybe you both need time to figure out who you are and love from a distance."

I was talking to the godfather of my kids, so I felt comfortable saying the next thing. I looked up at him. "I'm scared. I'm scared I'm going to raise unhappy kids because I chose to divorce."

Adam looked at me in the eyes. At that moment, he reached in the back of his mind and pulled out what had to be the most profound thing he'd ever said to me.

"What are you gonna do? Protect them from sadness, fear, and pain? Those are emotions. They're what God gave all of us, and they make us human. You're not putting them in a harmful environment if you decide to raise them by yourself. Your micromanaging, controlling ass will make sure they have everything they need. Sometimes it's better to raise kids who know how to recover from pain, so they can be a voice of comfort for others."

I shook my head, leaning into him for a hug. Which always hurt, because Adam is a bodybuilder, and his muscles often leave me feeling suffocated.

"Now I don't wanna talk about you anymore. Show me a picture of my god babies." He joked.

The next morning, I woke up feeling as if I'd slept 19 hours. I was refreshed and calm. It was the first morning I'd fully opened my eyes without them feeling swollen or in pain.

If this was what weed can do for a mama...huh. Maybe I should rethink this, I thought.

I rolled to my left and saw the back of a slender, caramel-colored woman with wild cinnamon hair in bed with me.

"Got dammit, Jayia! I said put on some clothes!" I yelled. "Got me thinking I woke up after getting high AND fucking a woman the night before!"

Jayia's naked shoulders moved up and down in laughter.

Chapter Eight
Rome Took How F***ing Long?

When you know yourself, you're less likely to lose yourself. Maybe you didn't know yourself in your early twenties.

Maybe you're getting to know yourself now.

I'M MARSHA MOTHERF***ING PARHAM AND DON'T YOU FORGET IT

H and me the vanilla, please."

James reached into the narrow kitchen cabinet by the sink.

"No, I don't keep it there anymore," I said. "It's in the cabinets closer to the stove."

My hands were wrist-deep in coconut milk, challah bread, and cinnamon sugar. I was preparing our annual Carter Bunch Christmas Brunch. Though we were still separated, I wanted to hold onto our family traditions. I'd been researching recipes for months that our family and friends would enjoy, purchasing all the gadgets I'd need to make each one. The full menu was sausage, shrimp and grits, chicken and cornbread waffles, glory muffins, fruit salad, cinnamon French toast, and bacon. (I hated the fact that every year everybody wanted bacon on the menu. There's no creativity involved with cooking that, but what the hell?)

Keeping the Christmas brunch alive was another way of me continuing to honor my grandmother's memory. She'd attended the first year I planned one, and it felt symbolic to turn it into a tradition the next year. Coincidentally, I'd also promised her at that first brunch that I would work on having a relationship with my mom, even though I didn't find it necessary (I was grown now).

I'd succumbed to the fact that my mission statement was trash, but still, I held on to the belief that if I followed Granny's life lessons, carrying them out with grace, insight, and tenderness, I could be more like her; wise and admirable. I supposed it wouldn't directly tie into my health, parenting, or marital goals, but it just seemed like a cool thing to be.

James handed me the vanilla, and it fell on the floor. Luckily, it was closed. I held out my hands. I hadn't even noticed they weren't steady.

James and I looked at one another, and I sighed. He went back to setting the dining room table, changing the unspoken subject. "I'm glad we settled on just putting the gifts from Santa under the tree this year instead of wrapping them."

I chuckled. "Me too! I DEFINITELY didn't have the time for that shit!" Apparently, in some homes, Santa wraps toys? Well, not in mine. He leaves them under the tree so kids can play with them immediately.

Our dynamic had changed these past few weeks. I was tired of being a mother to the people who were sliced out of my stomach, so you can imagine how much I was tired of being a mother to James. The exhaustion I'd felt from complaining about his lack of interest and scolding his actions when he did show interest had hit me. I had figured that once he wasn't in the house, it would be harder to parent solo. Without him at home, though, I'd been doing a lot less nagging.

What I didn't expect was how deeply I'd miss him as a friend. The inside jokes we shared, the way we both thought each other had the cutest, smartest kids on the planet, and the memories we'd made since college. James had changed since we'd gotten married, but I had too. It's been said that people enter your life for seasons, but I believe people have their own internal seasons as well. I guess that's a good thing. Put into perspective, if James weren't capable of change, I'd be married to an eight-year-old boy who watched Teenage Mutant Ninja Turtles and rode his bike to the corner store.

Maya walked through the dining room into the kitchen. I turned my head. "Hi, baby! You enjoy your new gifts from Santa?"

"YES!" She yelled. "Look at what I can do! Ommmmmmm," she closed her eyes and took a deep breath, putting her right foot above her left knee. Tree pose.

"Wow! Look at you, little yogi! Very cool. Can you set the table while Daddy grabs the serving trays so I can put the food on the table? I see your grandfather walking up the driveway right now, so people are coming," I asked hastily, ignoring the pose.

"Sure, Mommy!" she replied.

James grabbed the white china serving trays, placing them on the counter. He scooped the grits into a bowl and poured the shrimp and sausage dish on top. West peeked his head out of the family room and started to walk into the kitchen.

"Hold on one second, little man. I'm coming to play with you," he giggled to West. James put the dish on the dining room table and picked up West. They both went into the family room to play.

I smiled.

I turned my head and looked at the time: 9:43 a.m. Of course, my father was 17 minutes early. Of course. "Hi, Dad," I acknowledged him as he entered the back kitchen door.

"Well, hello there," he said, lifting his arm to show what appeared to be a bag from the grocery store. "I brought some orange juice to contribute to the festivity!" My dad took off his oversized leather jacket and strolled to a seat in the kitchen.

Chapter Nine
I'm Marsha Motherf***ing Parham And Don't You Forget It

"I tell you every year not to bring anything, but you don't listen. If you wanna bring something, bring me money for my student loans!" I joked.

"What? You have student loans? I thought your mother said you went to school for free," he joked back. His amnesia over the payment of my college education was an ongoing joke for over a decade between the two of us. Spoiler alert: I was still paying for that shit. And the joke was one that my bank account didn't find quite amusing.

"Hi, Grandpop!" Maya called from the living room. "I'm doing yoga, so I can't talk right now, but I'll be there in a second."

My dad laughed. "Okay, Maya. I'll just wait right here for you." He sat on the kitchen stool.

I moved from taking the waffles off the waffle iron, dropping the battered chicken into the deep fryer. Some of the grease popped onto my forearm, and though I saw it, I was working too fast to feel it.

"You like my new deep fryer?" I asked my dad.

"Very nice," he said.

"Good," I replied, wiping sweat from my forehead. "Now go into the family room with the boys. You're distracting me."

"Ok, ok," he laughed and carried his big ass bottle of orange juice into the family room.

As he exited the room, my back kitchen door opened again, and the alarm chimed. "Hello, Christine."

A chill ran down my back, making me stand straight as if I were a robot being commanded to engage.

"Hi, Ma. How are you?" My mother approached me, and our cheeks touched as if to greet each other with a kiss. Her ivory cheek was cold to the touch from the winter weather. Marsha removed her maroon suede coat, placing it next to my father's.

My stepfather Clyde was right behind her. "Heeyyy, Miss Christine!" he sang.

"Hi, Mr. Clyde," I smiled. I initially called him Mr. Clyde out of respect when I met him, but after they got married, I didn't stop. It had turned into a term of endearment.

Here we go, I whined as I poured the honey, cinnamon, and vanilla mixture over the fruit salad. I spilled some of the honey on my fingers, quickly searching for a paper towel.

Bring on the (Tom) Petty criticism, I thought. I know I was supposed to be kind to her because I promised Granny, but the divide between my mother and I couldn't be greater.

She stopped knowing who I was years ago. How could she (and why would she) possibly care to know who I am now?

My mother saw my latest article for *Parents* on the kitchen table, earmarked. My father must have opened the magazine and flipped through it while I was popping the muffins out from the cupcake pan.

"Is this your article?" she asked.

"Yes," I replied matter-of-factly.

"That's wonderful! Can I read it and have this copy?"

What the fuck? "Uhhh...yeah. Sure," I said. She'd caught me off guard with that.

My train of thought was interrupted by a shadowy figure that I saw out the corner of my eye. I believe the sky turned gray, and ominous clouds appeared as well, but I could be over-exaggerating.

My in-laws had arrived.

Chapter Nine
I'm Marsha Motherf***ing Parham And Don't You Forget It

"Merry Christmas," my mother and I sneered in unison flatly. I did love that about Marsha Parham. Business had taught us both the uncanny ability to remain polite at all times, even when surrounded by gargoyles.

"Are James and the kids in the other room?" my mother-in-law asked.

"Yes," I responded, again flatly.

"Is the food not ready?" she questioned, clearly watching me put the fried chicken on a serving platter.

"It is," I said. "I'm carrying everything to the table now." God forbid your evil ass help me carry something over to it.

After brunch, the men complimented me on a fantastic meal and got up one by one from their chairs. They headed along with the kids to the family room to watch *A Christmas Story*. My mother, mother-in-law, and I remained at the dining room table.

"So, Marsha, how are you?" Hagatha asked, probing for gossip.

"I'm well, and how are you?" Marsha replied immediately. She knew what was up.

"I'm well."

There we sat for a few moments in silence, each of us staring at something—anything other than each other—to avoid eye contact. Thankfully, Maya came back into the dining room to break the silence. She handed me my cell phone.

"Mommy, your phone made a sound," she said. She ran back out of the room.

I checked the phone and saw a Gmail notification. My *Forbes* editor had emailed me. I unlocked the phone, seeing he had sent me a message about my latest article. He asked me to make a slight correction. He'd profusely apologized in the email for sending it on a holiday but was hoping I could make the change as soon as possible.

"Excuse me for one second," I said. I got up from the table and started to head out of the room.

From the corner of my eye, I saw my mother-in-law readjust herself on the brown leather chair. The slight squeak was what caught my attention.

"That bitch is always working," I heard her mumble under her breath.

I stopped in my tracks, which made her realize her mumble was loud enough for my mother and me to hear. My mother looked at her directly in the eye this time.

"Excuse me?" Marsha asked, leaning into the table.

"I didn't say anything. Perhaps you misunderstood me."

"Well, which is it? You didn't say anything or I misunder—"

"You're the bitch." Only I didn't think it this time. I shrieked it.

In that brief moment of dialogue between my mother and my mother-in-law, I'd crossed the point of no return. I'd had enough. A pain shot through my clenched jaw. My hands shook, and my stomach started to rumble as if I was about to erupt.

And I did.

"YOU'RE THE BITCH!" I screamed. Not only did I repeat the phrase louder, but this time, James, my father-in-law, father, and the kids could hear me. I looked directly at my mother-in-law and continued loudly.

"AND YEAH, THIS BITCH IS ALWAYS WORKING. BECAUSE I'M TRYING TO GIVE MY KIDS SHIT YOU COULDN'T GIVE YOURS! AND THAT DOESN'T MAKE ME A BAD MOTHER, BY THE WAY. I CAN STILL SIT UP HERE

Chapter Nine
I'm Marsha Motherf***ing Parham And Don't You Forget It

AND COOK THIS AWESOME ASS MEAL AND LOVE MY KIDS. AND IF I GOTTA DO ALL THAT WITH OR WITHOUT YOUR SON'S BLACK ASS, THEN YEAH; I'LL BE A BAD BITCH."

I was so sick of this troll. I wanted a family, but she always felt the need to thwart my efforts. I tried to rescue her son, but she refused to allow it. Our extreme relationship may have been a thorn in my marriage, but I wasn't going to let it cost me my sanity.

Everyone in the house stared at me, surprised at my aggression toward Hagatha. I stood there in the silence, in between my kitchen and dining room doorway, where I was unable to move. Everyone looked back at me in shock but one person—Marsha Parham. She was grinning harder than the Sith Lord when Darth Vader took his first steps from the operating table.

My mother-in-law rolled her eyes and stood up from the dining room table. I squared up, fully prepared for her to do what she'd been waiting to do since the moment her son brought me home to meet her—punch me in the face. But she simply brushed past me and walked into the kitchen and out the back door. No one followed her.

"Just give her a minute," James replied from the family room couch. My dad shrugged his shoulders and continued watching the movie.

"Where did Maw Maw go?" Maya asked.

"She'll be back," James reassured her. "She's just going to the car." To more than likely grab a cigarette and hop on her cell phone, calling anyone who'd listen to how her daughter-in-law cursed her out on Christmas.

My mom stood up as well and grabbed her coffee cup. "C'mon. Let's you and I go sit on the couch in the living room by the fireplace."

She escorted me slowly around the corner past the stairs where we saw the Christmas tree. "Oh, how stunning, Chrissy. You really did an amazing job today."

My jaw started to tremble, and I kept blinking over and over. My shoulders dropped, and the tears began to fall.

"Oh, don't cry over that evil bitch," she said.

"I'm not crying over that, Ma," I responded. I realized I was at the point of no return. I wasn't validating my life for my mother-in-law anymore. I wasn't validating it for James, or even my mother. I was validating it for me.

"I'm just so tired," I told her as she continued walking me over to the couch. We sat.

"I know I went too far. I'm not sure if James and I will ever get back together, and especially now that I've cussed his momma out."

Marsha laughed, rubbing my back. I jumped at the touch initially, like a puppy whose master tried to pet them after a harsh scolding. We didn't have an intimate relationship. I didn't know how to respond to the touch, but at that moment, I found it comforting.

"She obviously knows our issues. He's been living with his parents, but she doesn't get it. Working and being married and raising kids is hard, and I'm trying..."

"You're excelling at it," my mother said. I looked up from staring at my lap and at her face. Marsha wiped the tears from my cheek with her thumb.

"I was in the same situation as you, and I didn't handle it nearly as well. I snapped on my kids constantly. I relied on your grandmother to raise you way more than you rely on me. Or even *can* rely on me. I'm still so busy traveling for work," she chuckled and continued. "And your father and I separated before you were even one, and the sight of the man still pisses me off."

I laughed.

"You and James were able to get together and put on this brunch. I know you did most of the work, but the fact that he's here and wanted

Chapter Nine
I'm Marsha Motherf***ing Parham And Don't You Forget It

to be here for you is incredible," she said. "You are, in fact, doing a good job, Christine. As you kids say, you're goals."

I laughed harder, wiping my own face. "Yeah, ok, Ma."

"You're not going to do all this perfectly," she said. "I didn't figure that out until this marriage and at fifty years old. We're all just learning this shit as we go, but I want you to accept that much sooner than I did."

My mother was right. I started looking back at all the things I needed help with that I didn't ask for—my marriage, my home, raising my kids, my health, and my time. I had shortcomings, but I started to believe I *was* my shortcomings and that I was a failure.

But oddly enough, at the same time, my desire to be perfect wouldn't allow me to course correct. I was "determined to improve all aspects of my life," yet unwilling to let my guard down and accept my flaws so that I could embody the changes.

In blocking myself, I'd become my own enemy.

Why did I do that? Marsha was saying she did the same thing, so why did she do that? Why were we holding onto a false perception of reality, feeling pressured to live our lives in a façade? Why did we feel as if we had something to prove?

My mother put her right arm around me and pulled me into her. I breathed deeply and sighed. My body relaxed, and I confessed something to her.

"I've been so stressed out lately; I've been texting that fool from my past just so I can have someone to talk to."

My mother replied without judgment. "Sometimes it feels good to talk to an old flame. It's a soft spot to lay your head. But just remember a soft spot to land on is not always the right spot to land on."

Did I low-key respect this woman? How similar *were* we? I thought about her advice, and you know what? She was right. It wasn't the man I admired, but the lifestyle and perspective that WOMANIZER had. Unlike me, he was willing to live life on his own terms and against societal expectations. Why the hell did it take me so long to *realize that?*

I hated Marsha Parham so bad for what I thought were mistakes she made as a mother; I built a false perception of reality in my marriage. I overcompensated in my career. I put all my eggs into the basket of a man who I thought would help me be the perfect wife, mom, and businesswoman. I felt pressured to live a façade. The marriage didn't make me happy. I loved James, and I knew he loved me too, but if we continued to stay married, it would only be because we felt we had something to prove.

Maybe I couldn't be like my grandmother. Perhaps I'd skipped a more relevant role model. Why did I spend so much time hating this woman? Not wanting to be this woman? How did I miss I was becoming this woman?

"You can't plan every detail of your life, baby. Every scenario. What if it goes well? What if it doesn't? What if you should stay married? What if you should get divorced? All you know is that planning too much for others got you to this point. Try feeling for you and see where that gets you."

I nodded in the crevasse of her cream-colored titties. She was right. It was time to be unapologetically myself, to give zero fucks and not care how I was perceived.

I was so busy trying to raise Maya how I wasn't raised that I forgot to sprinkle in a little bit of how I *was* raised. I needed to give Marsha Parham a fucking break. Being a working mother is always hard. There's always a new challenge that makes you feel like a first-time mom all over again. There is no perfect way to tackle any of this, and there are no straightforward answers. On-the-job training every day like a motherfucker.

Chapter Nine
I'm Marsha Motherf***ing Parham And Don't You Forget It

Maybe daughters are supposed to be a concentrated dose of their mothers. After all, I am of my mom.

I'm my mom AF.

We're all just learning this shit as we go, but **I** want you to accept that much sooner than **I** did.

CHAPTER TEN

THE UNEXPECTED EVOLUTION OF A BAD MOTHERF*****

6:20 AM: Get the kids dressed & James out the door! 👀💀

I turned to my iPhone on the bedside table. I needed to fix that alarm.

6:20 AM: Get the kids dressed & out the door! 👀💀

6:50 AM: Get the kids dressed & out the door! 👀💀

7:10 AM: Wake up

I wanted the extra damn time in the bed. Turning off the alarm, I looked at my inspirational thought of the day from one of my apps:

"Excuses fuel failure. No matter how hard you try to blame others for the events of your life, each event is the result of choices you made and are making."

I nodded, but turned off the phone and rolled back over. The slight breeze of the August morning felt good on my face. From my new apartment window downtown, I could see a woman walking her dog to the corner coffee shop and a man in a Ravens jersey eating a muffin.

An hour later, I was up and ready to start the day. We'd moved out of the "3,000 Square Foot House of Expectations" and into a three-bedroom apartment in downtown Baltimore. I walked into Maya's new room, where I saw her already dressed in a pink and magenta polka dot t-shirt, matched with lime green pants. I was so proud of how independent she'd become. Her vocabulary had grown, and she'd learned to ride a bike. She had also memorized her address and my cell phone number.

If I blinked, I would have missed all of that, but reconnecting with my mother these past eight months changed my attitude toward motherhood. I lived as much as I could in the moment with Maya, not multi-tasking when she talked to me. I also let her see how I included her in the work I did when she was not around. She always knew when Mommy was writing a parenting article or on her computer reading reports about kids her age. Then, she knew I was thinking of her. I still feel mom guilt, but now I acknowledge it, accept it and move the fuck on.

Maya's TV was playing Peppa Pig in the background, while she stomped and dug through her toy chest in the corner.

"I got myself all dressed this morning, Mommy! I'm ready, but I can't find my iPad cord! I'm so MAD!" Maya grunted and huffed.

'Baby, first of all, you can borrow my charger. Second, it's not that big a deal."

"It is! I put it over there, I thought..." she pointed to her bedside table, "and it's not there! AHHHH!"

"Maya, you're going to blow a gasket. What do we do when we're mad? Take a deep breath. Let's do it together. In. One."

We inhaled and exhaled.

"Two."

Again.

"And three. Wooooo. See how much calmer you feel now? You can borrow my charger, and we'll find yours later."

Oh yeah. I was on my elevated meditation shit as a mother now. It was an excellent decision to rethink the mission statement from last year, but I did want to keep one statement with me: your capacity to keep your vow will depend on the purity of your life. Not my words. Gandhi's.

These past several months made me realize how much of a tightly wound woman I was. It also made me realize how some of my anxiety and desire for control was rubbing off on my own daughter. So, I made it a point to stop trying to catch her before she fell. Instead, I focused on being present when the fall happened.

All of her milestones were incredible, but I could tell a self-imposed need to succeed was developing too. I didn't want her primary objective to be becoming a straight-A student, debutante, pageant queen, or all the things I felt compelled to do as a child to make my mom happy. I just wanted Maya to be comfortable in her own skin.

Still, I knew one thing for sure: the world didn't need another tightly wound, unhappy woman.

Maya was getting ready for a week with her dad. Lindsey and I decided to embark on our first momcation, a vacation just for mothers. James was on his way to pick up the kids and keep them for the week while I was away.

No children and no husbands. That last part wouldn't be hard for me! I felt like I'd finally found a way to try new things, but at the same time, I had to stay true to me. No ass fucking; no weed. Just strutting on the beach in my leopard.

Man, I'd had a crazy ass year!

Chapter Ten
The Unexpected Evolution of a Bad Motherf*****

I'd booked our three-day trip to Miami Beach a few months ago, and we had been texting about it at least once a week. "Are you going to wear a one-piece or let everything hang?" I asked Lindsey one week during our text message exchange.

"Hang 😊!" Lindsey replied.

"Then fuck it. I'm gonna do the same! Watch out, Shonda. This is my Year of Yes! LMFAOOO!"

"LOLOLOLOL," she replied. "Do you need to speak while we're down there?"

I'd always tried to schedule girl's trips on the back of one of my work trips. I'd speak at a conference and book an extra night for us to have fun. But we never ended up doing anything other than watching a Vanderpump Rules marathon in the hotel room, snuggled tightly under our own full beds. This time, though, I'd promised I'd come in on day one of a women in the workplace conference conference for a quick Q&A. After that, I'd be ready for a long momcation.

"Just a quick speaking gig then it's #HOTGIRLSUMMER!" I exclaimed through text.

Despite all my big talk, I knew we'd keep it pretty chill—massages, food crawls, and laying on the beach. No drinking birdie shots in the middle of a Cuban nightclub.

Well, *maybe* no drinking birdie shots in the middle of a Cuban nightclub. I was (technically) single, and it was still a hot girl summer. I was bringing back being selfish as a mother and woman, and it felt goooooood to put myself first.

I was on a journey to becoming confident in who I was, while I was learning to accept, trust, and love myself. Hell, sometimes even make love to me. (It wasn't like my controlling ass wanted to spend the time teaching another man what I liked and didn't like between the sheets. A bitch got kids and two full-time jobs.)

"Look at your nephew this morning eating his Cheerios. Isn't he cute?" Lindsey texted.

I had a revelation: Lindsey (and AJ too, for that matter) didn't live their lives to make me feel bad about mine. Maybe they weren't sharing photos of their cute kids and professing their love in public to show how perfect they were. Perhaps they were doing so in moments when everything wasn't perfect when they felt like shit. I could absolutely relate to that feeling. Every now and again, it's nice to go back to the highlight reel of our lives and remember the great moments. Why did it take me so long to realize that?

"Soooo cute. My love!" I replied to Lindsey.

"Mommy! Daddy's here! He's outside," Maya yelled, breaking my train of thought.

"I like you, Mommy," she continued. "You're nice. You work hard, but don't care so much."

This little Yoda I'd raised melted my heart every time. I helped Maya put each arm into her pink sequin backpack and kneeled, so we were face to face. I smiled and gave her a big kiss on the lips.

Hearing Maya's approval as my daughter made me think back to my childhood. My mother was always stressed, and I felt like I missed the mark with her expectations. It took me well into my adulthood to realize those two ideas aren't related, but I came to that realization after learning some tough life lessons. To this day, I wish for more carefree, laughter-filled moments with her as a child.

Fuck it, I shrugged. Since I'm clearly turning into my mom naturally, that means I must be raising myself through Maya too. Maybe God is laughing at me once again, telling me, "since you think you can do a better job, put your money where your mouth is and do it better." SMH.

If that was the case, I was gonna use the gift of time travel that I'd been given wisely. At her age, Maya didn't care whether or not I was

Chapter Ten
The Unexpected Evolution of a Bad Motherf*****

physically fit. I'm sure she couldn't give a damn about my sensual passion. I spent most of my marriage stressing out and putting pressure on myself in the name of being the perfect wife and mother, but Maya didn't care about any of that. She just wanted me to be happy because it made her happy.

At the end of this journey, I may not have hit the mark in guiding disciplined, gracious, educated, spiritual children as I had intended, but shit. People were gonna have opinions about how I raised the kids until they're 58 years old, anyway. But I did want to maintain a great relationship with them well into their adulthood. The best way for me to do that is to maintain a sense of who I am and what I need in life to be happy. And I'm gonna make damn sure that I'm a loving, present mother.

"Thanks, baby. Have fun with Daddy!" I grinned and kissed her forehead. I walked down the hall and opened the apartment door. James strolled down the hall. "I have a key, you know," he smiled.

"I know. I was just opening the door for you. Damn!" I joked. We were divorcing but hadn't been as happy as we were now with one another in a long time.

Well, I've been 'fraid of changin'...

built my life around you...time makes you bolder...

and I'm gettin' older, too

Brandon, the Uber driver from Miami International Airport to the hotel, was playing the hell outta one of my favorite songs, "Landslide" by Fleetwood Mac. I didn't appreciate it when I was younger, but now that Stevie Nicks was singing my life story, I told him to turn that shit up so I could sing along.

I clapped at the end of the song as the audience did in the live version and sighed. I turned to Lindsey, and she smiled while putting on mascara. "Are you ready to jump right out and speak?" She asked with concern.

"Girl, what's my motherfucking name?" I sassed, blotting my maroon lipstick with a fast food napkin Brandon handed me.

I thanked Brandon for the ride and opened the Uber app to give him five stars and a tip, off the strength of his music choices alone. We headed into the marble hotel lobby with our luggage and found a digital sign indicating where the conference was being held.

"I'm going to run to the bathroom but will meet you upstairs in the Q&A room," Lindsey said.

"Sounds good." I headed up the escalator to the conference and was told by the registration team to go ahead and head into the third room on the left. Brandon had great music choices but admittedly was a slow-ass driver, so I'd arrived at my Q&A session with just minutes to spare.

"And here she is...Christine Michel Carter!"

Yeesh...or so I *thought* I had minutes to spare. Shit. No worries.

The interviewer was so kind as to not call me out for being late when she introduced me. I left my luggage in the back of the room and walked up the middle aisle right onto the stage. I gave her a big hug and picked up my microphone from the seat I assumed was meant for me.

"Hi guys, thank you soooo much for coming to hear me speak! How are youuuuu?" I sang.

The audience smiled, forgiving my tardiness. Olivia, the interviewer, and I sat down and started the Q&A.

Olivia began, "Christine, I've already given the audience your bio, so I'm going to dig right in and ask you questions. I recently read a heartfelt post on your Instagram that you're separated from your husband."

Chapter Ten
The Unexpected Evolution of a Bad Motherf*****

"That's right, and getting divorced," I added. The audience quietly, but collectively, let out a sad sigh.

"It's alright, you guys," I laughed. "I always say I've never met an unhappy divorced woman, just a fed up one!"

The audience laughed. I'd lightened the mood, thank God.

Olivia continued, "How are you handling the separation?"

"Well," I reassured, "with the help of my family, friends, Jesus, and edibles."

The audience roared and cheered. I felt back in the professional swing of things, killing it amongst my tribe, who turned out to be a 420 audience of working moms. But it turns out I'd written off weed edibles too soon because those guys...deeeeffffinitely help me.

> "It's not that my husband wasn't family—he definitely was. But the past year, I've earned the true power and impact family has on us as spouses, mothers, professionals...it's incredible. I'm now drawing strength from the family I was born into and the family I've made from friends along the way."

Lindsey had made it to the room and was in the back waving. I winked at her and added:

> "The experience has caused me to reflect on the woman I wanted to model my life after, my grandmother. She never said she wanted me to be like her, of course, but she constantly asked me to make sure when she left the Earth that I had a good relationship with my own mother. Classic mother-daughter shit, that was not easy for me, you can imagine..."

Olivia and the audience laughed.

"But I think what my grandmother was indirectly teaching was that as women—particularly black women, and mothers—we draw our strength from family. Whether we use that strength to our benefit or detriment is up to us. Now in my life, I'm at a place where I'm so thankful for the friendships and conversations with women that made me feel normal. Those talks and relationships made me feel like I wasn't alone in choosing me so that I could become a better woman and mother."

The audience clapped, and I nodded, feeling the warmth in the room enter my soul.

Olivia summarized my rant. "You're finding comfort in being authentic to you, and you only, living your best life."

"Yassss cause I ain't going back and forth with you..." I joked, and the audience chuckled at the song reference.

"Am I perfect now? No. I'm still working on coming to an understanding of who I am. And I'm no Iyanla Vanzant, but I do think I've learned the power of a tribe, friendship, and women. My challenges have been given a purpose, and thanks be to God that I can use Him to help another mother or woman questioning her place in the world."

A woman in the audience cheered. I smiled at her; I wasn't trying to be overly spiritual, just honest. Candid. Making eye contact with her, I thought of all of the women I continued to meet who were struggling silently. Somehow, I felt compelled to keep telling their stories through my own.

"All of you look so fabulous today here in this room as boss babes. Yassss! But let's keep it real: so many of you are also drowning at home. This whole experience taught me that it's okay to say out loud to others that you don't

Chapter Ten
The Unexpected Evolution of a Bad Motherf*****

have everything together. It's okay to admit that you question where you are in your marriage, or how you're doing as a mom, or as a professional. It's the 21ˢᵗ century—there's no need to hold onto what things should look like for you."

Olivia nodded and asked me a follow-up question, "You mentioned boss babes. How does one balance work and home as a boss babe? As a mom?"

I sighed. Looking back, I firmly believed this concept contributed to my madness. I thought about all the statistics, facts and figures I could give in response. But I knew the answer I needed to give, and it needed to come from the heart.

> "Look—there are times that as women, we aren't spending as much time with our kids for work, and there are times when our work is pushed to the side because we need to walk away from the company, recharge, practice self-care and have time with our children. It always ebbs and flows. I'll never have it balanced as society thinks I should, but now I do try to bring my authentic self to my work and personal life. My children understand what I do and how hard I work, and my colleagues know I'm bringing the perspective of a working mom into our meetings, because that's what's most important to me. But at the end of the day when I think of work/life balance, I think of having it all. And I said during a recent keynote that the only way for a mom to have it all is to go to the store and buy a bottle of All detergent. And even that shit runs out."

The audience roared.

When I got back from Miami, Handsome McHandsomekins and I got to work on legally ending our marriage. We were so aligned on the divorce and custody process, it took us one hour to iron everything out. We downloaded a template separation and settlement agreement from the State of Maryland website, populating the entire document over a meat lover's pizza one night in the apartment while the children were sleeping.

(Oh, yeah. I'd *totally* stopped killing myself to eat healthy and go to the gym. And you know what? I was okay with it. I was working on a healthy mindset instead. At least that's what I told my back fat when I talked to it in the mirror.)

Filling in specific fields reminded us of hilarious moments in our relationship. "Ok, it says to list businesses, if any." James started to write the names of our small businesses and stopped. He looked at me and laughed. "Remember when you fired your mom from your consulting firm when you first started it?" He kept smiling.

"Yes, I did," I said, dipping my pizza crust in the garlic butter. "And I'd do it again because she wasn't dedicated to the company. Filling out forms late and shit."

We chuckled.

"You are so controlling," James chuckled.

"And you know this, maaannn!" I replied.

James smiled and then got serious for a moment. "You know, that's not always a bad thing." He put his hand over my hand that wasn't stuffing pizza down my throat. I turned, my mouth open mid-bite as I looked at him. "It just wasn't a fit for us as a couple."

I nodded, my cheeks full. James smiled and went back to completing the forms, pausing to sip some of his Pepsi. If only marriage was as easy as the wedding day. If they say the biggest statement and testimony of your devotion to your spouse is the last day of marriage (not the first), then I was very proud of James and I. At the beginning of our marriage, I wouldn't dare let anyone speak to James in a condescending or criticizing tone, but that's how I spent most of our

Chapter Ten
The Unexpected Evolution of a Bad Motherf*****

marriage talking to him. I thought he was always making mistakes until I stepped back and realized...guess what?

So were you, Christine.

"We were raised differently. We brought different viewpoints and experiences into our marriage." I reassured him.

James thought for a minute, pulling a slice of pizza from the box. "Maybe you wouldn't have felt like you needed to do everything if I helped more and got that old school way of thinking out my head."

I shrugged.

I was learning to accept the way James contributed to the household. Strange to say that he had to leave home to add to it, but hey. He was raised in a family with Hagatha where he didn't learn how to be a "man of the house." And I wasn't sure if I'd married him to save him from that household, or if I had wanted someone to control. But I was learning to patiently let him help in the way that he knew how. As a result, he was on a journey to discovering what that meant for him.

People are multifaceted and sensitive. Not women, but people. It took me wayyyy too long to learn that fact. James carried his shortcomings with him, and the burden of his shortcomings manifested in his depression and alcoholism. We'd both brushed too much under the rug in our marriage in search of a perfect life. I'd spent too much time pointing the finger at him (not realizing three were pointing back at me). I'd ignored him too often when he claimed he was tired and going to the basement and when he showed disinterest in participating in activities with me and the kids.

I was proud of him for seeking help for his depression over the past few months instead of hiding it. Depression can affect any man and father at any age. Thankfully, he was getting better as a result of honest conversations with me and our therapist, along with environmental changes and prescribed medications. He was once again becoming interested in his work, his family, and himself.

I thought I wanted my husband to be just like me to complement me until I realized that, by definition, isn't complementary. It's identical. I learned I needed someone who understood me (and might even help me escape myself so that I could be a saner version of me when I returned).

James chuckled. "We sure did turn into horrible lovers. It's amazing we lasted as long as we did!"

I died laughing in agreement and sighed. "It's crazy how we had to stop being a husband and wife so we could become a better man and woman."

We weren't the same people we were when we got married. Hell, in another five years, we'd be entirely new people again. We'd moved from a state of doubt and sadness, evolving back into being best friends. And we chose to be dedicated to one another differently. Together, we'd decided we weren't going to dwell on the past or fear the future. We were dealing with uncomfortable conversations in the present to lead to us being comfortable in the future. And no, we didn't give up while others chose to stick it out. We were making the right decision for us—for our family.

James stapled the paperwork and put it inside a manila envelope.

"For the record, I felt like I was stifling you. I didn't try to get back together because I realized I wasn't good for you. I have a lot to work on with the drinking and my own issues. It wasn't right to bring that into our marriage thinking they would magically fix themselves overnight."

I thought about his comment, and realized that taking on James' depression and alcoholism and trying to solve his problems *was* holding me back. It had affected my relationship with my children. I'd spent too much time being an authoritative figure in his life.

Looking back on those nights I spent uncontrollably (yet silently) crying in my bed for James I realized that although I wanted to feel like I was controlling everything around me, I was terrified to indeed be the sole person in control of my life. I'd made James my audience—the person I expected to applaud for me. He was there to give me brownie points when I mastered every one of my "working mom" tasks all alone. But I also made him my scapegoat, someone to blame if things went wrong. Albeit wrong, that was James. In those night hours, I was also furious he wasn't willing to fight for me; to show me the love I needed. Now, I realized, *why would a scapegoat feel as if they were ever genuinely wanted or needed?*

I stared at James, getting lost in thought. The thought of divorcing James and living my life for others' expectations no longer kept me up at night. Co-parenting was a welcomed anxiety. Hell, I'd already lived the alternative to it! I gave up grieving the marriage. In fact, I think I gave up grieving the marriage while we were still together. But I felt like I finally saw the light at the end of the tunnel, and my grief for our initial bond was disappearing.

"Hey," I asked James as he looked up. "You happy?"

"Yes." Handsome McHandsomekins smiled and gave me a kiss on the lips.

The road ahead of me looked marvelous. There were no guardrails, and there was only room for one car on it. I planned to forgive myself for the wrong stops I made along the way while just owning my shit—the good and the bad.

"I'm happy too."

I thought I wanted my husband to be just like me to complement me until I realized that, by definition, isn't complementary. It's identical.

Chapter Ten
The Unexpected Evolution of a Bad Motherf*****

Chapter Ten
The Unexpected Evolution of a Bad Motherf*****

EPILOGUE

THE BLACK MOMBA

I sat in front of my laptop and whined, "Is this something I have to do? I'm perfectly fine being a badass mom and businesswoman. My kids and career give me all the love I need."

"But who—I ask—is gonna take you out on dates, show you companionship—" Christopher was interrupted by Jayia.

"And fuck you!" She laughed, twerking, and rocking the dining room table with her ass. My brother and I winced, disgusted by her candor.

"Shit, I don't know how to do this, the last time I was single, Barack Obama wasn't even president!" I cried out. "I can't date in y'alls Trump era, getting catfished and murdered and what not!"

"Listen you old fart, you're still in your 30s. It's time for you to come into the digital age," Christopher berated, turning my laptop from facing me to him. "We're doing this, and dare I say it oh my God— It's going to be a new experience for you." He started typing.

"Oh, go to hell," I snapped.

"Oooo, this is exciting," Jayia smiled. "Not only is dating a new chapter for you as an adult but doing so as a mom...Maya and West are going to give these men the BLUES!" Jayia and Christopher looked at each other and pursed their lips.

"What the fuck ever," I gave up. "Let's just do this."

During our debate about whether I should set up of my online dating profile, Christopher had taken matters into his own hands, keyed in the necessary information and created a profile for me. "All you need to do is give me a few sentences about yourself and a username."

I struggled to think of what to say about myself. Describing me in a nutshell for work was something I could so quickly. My elevator pitch to convince a man to take me to Ruth Chris? Not so much. I repeated some of the phrases we'd already said in conversation.

"Uhhh, single divorced, successful businesswoman and mother looking for companionship. Enjoys eating.."

Jayia interrupted me, "fine dining."

I continued, "spending time with her babies—"

Jayia interrupted again, her raspy voice demanding, "Take that out, Christopher."

Christopher backspaced all my sentences. "Jayia and I will do it."

"Hella sexy..."

AHHH! I thought to myself. "Don't put that!" I yelled. Jayia continued, blocking me from reaching my brother with the laptop.

"...hella single, hella successful mom who hasn't dated in years. Knock the dust off boys. I'm not looking for a commitment as I'm focused on my career, but I'm ready to meet the man who will make me change my mind...at least for a moment."

I was mortified. Mortified at the fact that my siblings were setting me up with an online dating profile; mortified at the fact that I'd never truly been single in my life; and mortified at the fact that I didn't know how to describe myself or my interests outside of work and my children.

Christopher interrupted my train of thought. "Alright and...done. Just need to add a username to this."

"I want it to make it clear that I'm a mom got dammit. Shit," I chided.

"And I want it to show that you are a sexy, seductive, almost deadly captivating ass black woman. Don't worry, we'll get them damn kids in there somehow," Jayia dismissed and grinned.

Christopher smiled as he typed the username and turned the laptop to face me so I could see the complete profile.

Fine. But I'm not gonna take this shit seriously. "Bring it on boys, I guess," I smirked.

It was there, at my dining room table with my siblings, that I started my new adventure as a divorced millennial mom dating in her 30s, stuck between the courting practices of yesteryear and the hookup dick pic culture of the 21st century.

@theblackmomba was born.

ACKNOWLEDGMENTS

THANKS, GUYS!

I've got a bomb ass team.

It was vital for me to have this book handled start to finish by women—black women, and mothers at that. To the talented professional and mom Aja Dorsey Jackson, I needed you as a sounding board and editor to make sure I was telling an authentic story. To my dear Renee Hollingshead—you worked some sort of twisted alchemy in Photoshop on my mom bod for this cover. Shanna Sarsin, my publisher—thank you for seeing the vision and your genuine excitement in MOM AF. I was fed up with people telling me "this audience won't read your story;" "you're not important enough to write a book;" and watering down my narrative. You didn't do any of that and supported me from the moment we met.

Guys, you da real MVPs. Thank you so, so much. It DEFINITELY takes a village.

To the men and women (not just the mothers) who have:

- read every blog post;

- read every article;

- read every social media caption I've ever written; and

- listened to me ramble during every podcast interview, presentation, and speaker session:

I thank you and appreciate your support so very much. Words can't express how comforting it is for me to feel welcome in many rooms because of you before I even step in the door. Always feel like you can message me and share your stories. I'm saving them a hundred percent of the time while figuring out a way to collect your thoughts and amplify your voice to the masses. Even if we haven't met, you're one of my friends. :)

To the friends I've made since my days of playing in the alley on Cold Spring Avenue in Park Heights, Baltimore, Maryland—my eyes are swelling just thinking about all of you. God has blessed me along the way with such incredible, impactful friends. He also blessed me when he made me a lifelong resident of Baltimore—the greatest city in America. He gave me an entire community to laugh with, fight with, cry with, and everything in-between. I can't believe how lucky I am to have you supporting my every move.

To my family (immediate and extended, which includes some of the friends I'm thinking about above). I am who I am, and who I am destined to be, because of your love. Your supportive asses proofread content, work my events, and serve as quasi-publicists. I don't deserve you. But you've also taught me that a duality lives in me. I'm neither good nor evil. I am sexual. I am funny. I am kind. I am smart. I am prissy Chrissy. :) You've taught me to just be me, and all of me. My love for all of you runs beyond measure. I pray for people who don't have the love of close family members like I do. I'd do everything and anything it takes to keep you guys happy and safe. Please, please understand—my family is everything to me. That's all we have at the end of the day, and because I have you, I'm rich as fuck. :)

My parents argue constantly. They are opinionated, control freaks, and stubborn. But my parents are the most fascinating people on the planet. My only regret in life is that I learned at a late age how remarkable every facet of them truly is. They're both invaluable to me. It's because of them that I learned the importance of maintaining a common goal with your spouse, even after divorce. I'll never stop being proud to be your daughter. You both truly live life unapologetically on your own terms. Thank you for inspiring me, whether you think it is for the good or the bad. (Spoiler alert: it was always for good.)

And last, but certainly (and never) least, my ex-husband James Carter. You are a talented, loving powerhouse. I didn't always cherish you as the blessing you were during our marriage. In honoring and acknowledging you here, I also honor our little monsters. We're divorced, but I hope you never forget that you were my very best friend. I loved you so intensely and so deeply that I let you go. That was how I thanked God for my blessing; the only way I could truly show you how much I love you, Handsome McHandsomekins. You taught me devotion to a human being, and a more profound love and bond through children that no one can penetrate. You weren't ready to be a husband, and I wasn't prepared to sacrifice who I was to be your wife. But our love was genuine. Thank you for urging me to tell my story and to tell our story. Thank you for being okay with me sharing the good, bad, and ugly. I pray every night for your health and happiness. I hope you find what you need in this world.

Oh, wait! Beyoncé!

In all moments of praise, we must thank our Suga Mama, who art in L.A. or NYC, hallowed be thy sweet ass frame. Thank you for being such an inspiration. We don't deserve you, and by we, I mean black women, black men, and humanity periodt. I love you, girl. If I ever meet you, I'm gonna be like Jerome was all over Pam Grier, singing, "I Wanna Get Next to You" at the Players Ball.

Yes, Kenneth Epps and Marsha Parham, I took the time to make a special paragraph about Beyoncé but didn't call you out independently. Deal with it. (You'll both have a problem with that, proving you are, in fact, just alike.)

:)

That's everybody!

All my love,

Christine

Acknowledgments
Thanks, Guys!

Printed in Great Britain
by Amazon